Cambridge Proficiency
Examination Practice 1

Cambridge Proficiency

Examination Practice 1

Edited by Leo Jones for the University of Cambridge Local Examinations Syndicate

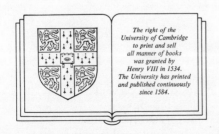

The right of the
University of Cambridge
to print and sell
all manner of books
was granted by
Henry VIII in 1534.
The University has printed
and published continuously
since 1584.

Cambridge University Press
Cambridge
London   New York   New Rochelle
Melbourne   Sydney

Published by the Press Syndicate of the University of Cambridge
The Pitt Building, Trumpington Street, Cambridge CB2 1RP
32 East 57th Street, New York, NY 10022, USA
10 Stamford Road, Oakleigh, Melbourne 3166, Australia

© Cambridge University Press 1984

First published 1984
Fifth printing 1986

Printed in Great Britain
at the Bath Press, Avon

ISBN 0 521 27425 7 Student's Book
ISBN 0 521 27426 5 Teacher's Book
ISBN 0 521 26356 5 Set of 2 cassettes

HE

Contents

Thanks

Thanks are due to the many collaborators who contributed to these materials and in particular to Richard Alderson, Lois Arthur, Sheila Condon, John Cowley, Frank Chaplen, Heather Daldry, Diana Fried-Booth, Patrick Gribben, Kathy Gude, Louise Hashemi, Tony Hopwood, Christian Kay, Roy Kingsbury, Ivor Levinson, Susan Morris, S. O'Connell, Raymond Pinder, Christopher Ross, Roger Scott, Alan Stanton, Wendy Stott, Jeff Stranks, Vivienne Ward, Pauline Werba, and to the Test Development and Research Unit.

To the student

This book is for candidates preparing for the University of Cambridge Certificate of Proficiency in English examination and provides practice in all the written and oral papers. It contains 5 complete tests, each of which is exactly like the examinations which will be set from June 1984; that is, incorporating the modifications of syllabus described by the University of Cambridge Local Examinations Syndicate in their booklet, *Cambridge Examinations in English Changes of Syllabus in 1984*. The official specimen papers included by the Syndicate in the booklet make up the first test in this book. The examination consists of 5 papers, as follows:

Paper 1 Reading Comprehension (1 hour)
> *Section A* consists of 25 multiple-choice items in the form of a sentence with a blank to be filled by 1 of 4 words or phrases.
> *Section B* consists of 15 multiple-choice items based on three or more reading passages of different types.

Paper 2 Composition (2 hours)
> There are 5 topics from which you choose 2. The topics include discursive and descriptive essays, a directed writing exercise and an essay based on optional reading. (In these practice tests the questions based on optional reading are set on the kind of books that are prescribed each year. These are not the actual books prescribed for any particular year: they are just given as examples.)

Paper 3 Use of English (2 hours)
> *Section A* contains exercises which test your control of English usage and grammatical structure.
> *Section B* consists of a passage followed by questions which test your comprehension and skill in summarising.

Paper 4 Listening Comprehension (about 30 minutes)
> You answer a variety of questions on recorded passages (normally 4) from English broadcasts, interviews, announcements, phone messages and conversations. Each passage is heard twice.

Paper 5 Interview (about 15 minutes)
> *Section A* is a conversation based on a photograph you are given to look at.
> *Section B* is a short reading passage. You are given time to read it through and identify the context before reading it aloud.
> *Section C* is a structured communication activity. You take part in a conversation or discussion with a group of other candidates or with the examiner alone. The exercises in these tests include some of the type set in the examination on optional reading.

[1]

Practice Test 1

PAPER 1   READING COMPREHENSION   (1 hour)

This paper is in two parts, section A and section B. For each question you answer correctly in section A you gain **one** *mark; for each question you answer correctly in section B you gain* **two** *marks. No marks are deducted for wrong answers. Answer all the questions. Indicate your choice of answer in every case on the separate sheet which should show your name and examination index number. Follow carefully the instructions about how to record your answer.*

SECTION A

In this section you must choose the word or phrase which best completes each sentence. For each question, 1 to 25, indicate on your answer sheet *the letter A, B, C or D against the number of the question.*

1   He couldn't .... his father that he was telling the truth.
    A admit   B confide   C trust   D convince

2   It was difficult to guess what her .... to the news would be.
    A feelings   B reaction   C capital   D opinion

3   In order to buy his house he had to obtain a large .... from his bank.
    A loan   B finance   C capital   D debt

4   My passport .... last month, so I will have to get a new one.
    A elapsed   B expired   C ended   D terminated

5   The Department is also deeply .... in various improvement schemes.
    A connected   B entailed   C involved   D implied

6   His answer was so confused that I could hardly make any .... of it at all.
    A interpretation   B meaning   C intelligibility   D sense

7   The main attraction of the job was that it offered the .... to do research.
    A possibility   B proposal   C opportunity   D prospect

8   I wish you'd tell me what I .... do in this difficult situation.
    A shall   B would   C should   D ought

[2]

9 A competitor may submit any number of entries .... each one is
   accompanied by a packet top.
   A supposing   B notwithstanding   C assuredly   D provided

10 They always kept on good .... with their next-door neighbours for the
    children's sake.
    A friendship   B relations   C will   D terms

11 He earns his living by .... old paintings.
    A reviving   B restoring   C reforming   D replenishing

12 Hotel rooms must be .... by noon, but luggage may be left with the
    porter.
    A vacated   B evacuated   C abandoned   D left

13 The majority of nurses are women, but in the higher ranks of the medical
    profession women are in a ....
    A rarity   B minority   C scarcity   D minimum

14 Although he was under no .... the shopkeeper replaced the defective
    battery free of charge.
    A urgency   B guarantee   C obligation   D insistence

15 Old Mr Brown's condition looks very serious and it is doubtful if he will
    ....
    A pull through   B pull up   C pull back   D pull out

16 To be a good short story writer one needs, among other things, a very
    .... imagination.
    A vivid   B living   C bright   D sparkling

17 This ticket .... you to a free meal in our new restaurant.
    A confers   B entitles   C grants   D credits

18 He was completely .... by the thief's disguise.
    A taken away   B taken down   C taken in   D taken through

19 This book gives a brief .... of the history of the castle and details of the
    art collection in the main hall.
    A outline   B reference   C article   D research

20 Mark is very set in his ways, but John has a more .... attitude to life.
    A changeable   B flexible   C moveable   D fluid

21 The BBC tries to .... for all tastes with its four national programmes.
    A suit   B furnish   C regard   D cater

22 It won't .... matter if you arrive a few minutes late.
    A greatly   B largely   C grandly   D considerably

23 All three TV channels provide extensive .... of sporting events.
    A vision   B coverage   C broadcast   D network

24 .... I am aware, there were no problems during the first six months.
    A As far as   B So much as   C Much more than   D Except that

25 The overcrowded living conditions .... a heavy strain on the family.
    A set   B put   C made   D pressed

SECTION B

In this section you will find after each of the passages a number of questions or unfinished statements about the passage, each with four suggested answers or ways of finishing. You must choose the one which you think fits best. For each question, 26 to 40, indicate on your answer sheet the letter A, B, C or D against the number of the question.

FIRST PASSAGE

I think it was De Mandeville who suggested a river party for the staffs of the various embassies. Nor, on the face of it, was the idea a bad one. All winter long the logs come down the River Sava until the frost locks them in: now with the spring thaw the east bank of the river has a pontoon of tree-trunks some forty feet wide lining the bank under the willows so that you can walk out over the river, avoiding the muddy margins, and swim in the deep water.

These logs had been made into a raft about a hundred feet by sixty – big enough even to dance on. While everyone was dancing the rumba and while the buffet was plying a heavy trade, it was noticed that the distance between the raft and the shore had noticeably increased. The gang-plank subsided in the ooze. It was not a great distance – perhaps ten feet. But owing to the solid resistance such a large raft set up in the main current the pull was definitely outward. But as yet nobody was alarmed; indeed most of the party thought it was part of a planned entertainment.

As we approached the next bend of the river it looked as if the whole thing would run aground on the bank, and a few of us made preparations to grab hold of the overhanging willows and halt our progress. But by ill luck a change in the current carried us just too far into the centre of the river and we were carried past the spit of land, vainly groping at the tips of bushes.

It was about another five minutes before the full significance of our position began to dawn upon us. By this time we were moving in stately fasion down the centre of the river, all lit up like a Christmas tree. Exclamations, suggestions, counter-suggestions poured from the lips of the diplomats and their wives in a dozen tongues.

Unknown to us, too, other factors were being introduced which were to make this a memorable night for us all. Spy-mania was at its height and the Yugoslav forces lived in a permanent state of alertness. There were frequent rumours of armed raids from Czechoslovakia.

It was in this context that some Yugoslav infantryman at an observation post along the river saw what he took to be a large armed man-of-war full of Czech paratroops in dinner jackets and ball-dresses sailing upon Belgrade. He did not wait to verify this first impression. He galloped into Belgrade castle a quarter of an hour later on a foam-flecked mule with the news that the city was about to be invaded.

26 A river party was practicable because
   A the river was lined with willow trees.
   B the banks were not muddy at this time.
   C there was a suitable surface for walking on.
   D there was not too much frost at this season.

27 The raft started moving from the shore because
   A the gang-plank had fallen in the mud.
   B the buffet was too heavy.
   C it stuck out too far.
   D the organisers wanted to surprise the guests.

28 The raft did not stop at the next bend because
   A there was too much mud on the river bank.
   B there were only bushes to catch hold of.
   C the current made it swirl outwards.
   D the water was not shallow enough.

29 The occupants of the raft were
   A completely unaware of their situation.
   B quarrelling in various languages.
   C indignant with the organisers of the party.
   D anxious to help solve the problem.

30 They came under suspicion because
   A the Yugoslavs feared an invasion.
   B Czechoslovakia was at war.
   C the country was full of spies.
   D of the way they were dressed.

31 The Yugoslav look-out made a mistake because
   A the party were dressed in soldiers' uniforms.
   B the raft was sailing towards Belgrade.
   C many of the party were armed.
   D he was affected by the general tension.

[5]

SECOND PASSAGE

A child who has once been pleased with a tale likes, as a rule, to have it retold in identically the same words, but this should not lead parents to treat printed fairy stories as sacred texts. It is always much better to tell a story than to read it out of a book and, if a parent can produce an improvement on the printed text, so much the better.

A charge made against fairy tales is that they harm the child by frightening him or arousing his sadistic impulses. To prove the latter, one would have to show in a controlled experiment that children who have read fairy stories were more often guilty of cruelty than those who had not. On the whole, their symbolic verbal discharge seems to be rather a safety valve than an incitement to overt action. As to fears, there are, I think, well-authenticated cases of children being dangerously terrified by some fairy story. Often, however, this arises from the child having been told the story on only one occasion. Familiarity with the story by repetition turns the pain of fear into the pleasure of a fear faced and mastered.

There are also people who object to fairy stories on the grounds that they are not objectively true, that giants, witches, two-headed dragons, magic carpets, etc., do not exist; and that, instead of indulging his fantasies in fairy tales, the child should be taught how to adapt to reality by studying history and mechanics. I find such people, I must confess, so unsympathetic and peculiar that I do not know how to argue with them. If their case were sound, the world should be full of madmen attempting to fly from New York to Philadelphia on a broomstick or covering a telephone with kisses in the belief that it was their enchanted girlfriend.

No fairy story ever claimed to be a description of the external world and no sane child has ever believed that it was.

32 The author considers that a fairy story is more effective when it is
  A   repeated without variation.
  B   treated with reverence.
  C   adapted by the parent.
  D   set in the past.

33 According to the passage great fear can be stimulated in a child when a story is
  A   full of cruelty.
  B   heard only once.
  C   repeated too often.
  D   dramatically told.

34 The advantage claimed for repeating fairy stories to young children is that it
  A   makes them come to terms with their fears.
  B   develops their power of memory.
  C   convinces them there is nothing to be afraid of.
  D   encourages them not to have ridiculous beliefs.

35 The author's mention of broomsticks and telephones is meant to suggest that
   A fairy stories are still being made up.
   B there are different kinds of truth.
   C fairy stories are different from reality.
   D there is more concern for children's fears nowadays.

THIRD PASSAGE

Extract 1

A stylish dining room with cream walls and curtains and black carpet as foil to an eclectic array of furniture. Many of the pieces are classics of their particular era, and demonstrate how old and new designs can be happily mixed together. The prototype chair in the foreground has yet to prove its staying power and was thought up by the flat's occupant. He is pictured in his living area which has the same decorative theme and is linked to the dining room by a high Medieval-styled archway where there was once a redundant and uninspiring fireplace.

Extract 2

Old bathrooms often contain a great deal of ugly pipework in need of disguising. This can either be done by boxing in the exposed pipes, or by fitting wood panelling over them.

As wood panelling can be secured over almost anything – including old ceramic tiles and chipped walls – it is an effective way of disguising pipework as well as being an attractive form of decoration. The panelling can be vertical, horizontal or diagonal.

An alternative way to approach the problem of exposed pipes is to actually make them a feature of the room by picking the pipework out in bright strong colours.

Extract 3

Cooking takes second place in this charming room which, with its deep armchairs, is more of a sitting room than a kitchen, and the new Rayburn stove was a good choice, as it blends in well with the old brick and beamed fireplace. There are no fitted units or built-in appliances, so all food preparation is done at the big farmhouse table in the foreground, and the china, pots and pans have been deliberately left on show to make an attractive display. What about the kitchen sink? It's hidden away behind an archway which leads into a small scullery. Here there's a second cooker and – in the best farmhouse tradition – a huge, walk-in larder for all food storage.

>>>>→

36 Why is the colour of the carpet described in extract 1 a particular
    advantage?
    A   It livens up the colour in an otherwise dull room.
    B   It provides a contrast to the furniture.
    C   It blends in with the tones of the furniture.
    D   It gives the room a classical style.

37 What is the purpose of the archway described in extract 1?
    A   To hide an unattractive fireplace.
    B   To give the room an exotic eastern style.
    C   To join the dining room with the sitting room.
    D   To make room for the unusual seating arrangements.

38 Extract 2 is probably taken from
    A   an architect's journal.
    B   a plumber's manual.
    C   a do-it-yourself magazine.
    D   an advertisement for new bathrooms.

39 Extracts 2 and 3 deal with
    A   concealing old furniture.
    B   attractive colour schemes.
    C   cheap improvement schemes.
    D   picking out decorative features.

40 Compared with extract 1 the room described in extract 3 appears
    to
    A   possess a greater variety of style.
    B   be more comfortable.
    C   be more colourful.
    D   contain more furniture.

PAPER 2 COMPOSITION (2 hours)

*Write **two only** of the following composition exercises. Your answers must follow exactly the instructions given. Write in pen, not pencil. You are allowed to make alterations, but see that your work is clear and easy to read.*

1 Write a descriptive account of a visit to a crowded beach. (About 350 words)

2 Write a balanced discussion on the theme 'A woman's place is in the home.' You may write in the form of a dialogue between two speakers, or in essay form. (About 350 words)

3 Describe the achievement and influence of any important compatriot of yours. (About 200 words)

4 You are Mr Pungent, who has just returned from the holiday abroad described in your telegram below. Write the promised letter to your local Travel Agent. Your answer should not exceed 200 words.

INCREDIBLE DELAY AIRPORT NO HOTEL TRANSPORT. ROOMS FOOD SERVICE SERIOUSLY SUBSTANDARD. GOOD HALF HOUR FROM SEA IN RUNDOWN NEIGHBOURHOOD. TOURS COURIER AND OTHER EXTRAS NON-EXISTENT. BROCHURE MISLEADING TO FRAUDULENT EXTENT. INSIST ON COMPLETE REFUND OR ELSE. LETTER FOLLOWS. G. PUNGENT.

5 Basing your answer on your reading of the prescribed text concerned, answer *one* of the following. (About 350 words)

SHAKESPEARE: *Hamlet*
'Seems Madam? nay, it is: I know not seems.' Explain how characteristic this line is of Prince Hamlet's character and attitudes.

HARDY: *Far From the Madding Crowd*
What underlying view of life do you find in this book, and how is it expressed?

KATHERINE MANSFIELD: *The Garden Party and Other Stories*
It is said that the key feature of Katherine Mansfield's art is to leave something important unstated, or only hinted at. Consider two of the stories in this collection as illustrations of this method of writing.

PAPER 3   USE OF ENGLISH   (2 hours)

SECTION A

1   *Fill each of the numbered blanks in the following passage with* **one** *suitable word.*

About three years .... , (1) in my mid-forties, I had a sudden and severe mental breakdown. There was nothing unusual about the breakdown itself, ... (2) about the events in my own life that .... (3) up to it. The .... (4) exceptional feature was that I am .... (5) psychologist and should therefore be able to view the events of my illness .... (6) two standpoints; subjectively as the patient and .... (7) objectively as the detached professional observer.

Until I broke down I .... (8) always regarded .... (9) as reasonably well-balanced: .... (10) I had sometimes worried .... (11) physical illness, ... (12) thought that I might be subjected .... (13) the torture and humiliation of a severe mental illness had never entered my head. .... (14) many years I had .... (15) outgoing, efficient, continually active and reasonably cheerful: I .... (16) of myself as well-meaning, ... (17) possibly somewhat insensitive .... (18) to my own and others' feelings. .... (19) never occurred to me that one day my existence would disintegrate .... (20) the space of a few hours.

2   *Finish each of the following sentences in such a way that it means exactly the same as the sentence printed before it.*

EXAMPLE: I expect that he will get there by lunchtime.

ANSWER: I expect him *to get there by lunchtime.*

[10]

a) 'You stole the jewels!' the inspector said to him.

The inspector accused ....

b) If it doesn't rain soon, millions of pounds' worth of crops will be lost.

Unless ....

c) 'Don't move or I'll shoot!' the bank robber said to the clerk.

The bank robber threatened ....

d) The drama critic of the 'Daily News' regards the new play as a major breakthrough.

According to ....

....

e) Although the team played well, they lost.

Despite ....

f) Galileo is considered to be the father of modern astronomy.

Galileo is regarded ....

g) The only way you can become a good athlete is by training hard every day.

Only by ....

h) He speaks more persuasively than his brother.

He is a ....

3 *Fill each of the blanks with a suitable word or phrase.*

EXAMPLE: Even if I had stood on a chair, *I wouldn't have been able to reach the light bulb.*

a) 'Have another cup of tea?'

'No, thank you. I've .... already.'

b) Seldom .... below zero in March, even in the mountains.

c) 'What .... ?' 'For stealing his firm's money, I think.'

d) Difficult ...., it is not completely impossible.

e) He took his car to the garage .... it repaired.

f) 'I've got toothache.'

   'You'd .... to the dentist's.'

4 *For each of the sentences below, write a new sentence as similar as possible in meaning to the original sentence, but using the words given in bold letters. The words must **not be altered** in any way.*

   EXAMPLE: John inflated the tyres of his bicycle.
   blew

   ANSWER: *John blew up the tyres of his bicycle.*

   a) I suffered from obsessive and agonising thoughts.
   prey

   ....

   b) He can hardly read at all.
   virtually

   ....

   c) He can speak French well enough to go to the conference.
   fluent

   ....

   d) His arrival was completely unexpected.
   took

   ....

   e) The first sign of the disease is a feeling of faintness.
   onset

   ....

   f) He began by giving us a summary of his progress so far.
   outset

   ....

   g) As an antidote to their disappointment, he bought them ice-cream.
   offset

   ....

h) I travel by bus only when I have no alternative.
resort

....

SECTION B

5   *Read the following passage, then answer the questions which follow it.*

In our village pub a man was eating a thick slice of elver cake. He was
enjoying it very much but he did not know what he was eating, because as
he munched away he indignantly denied that elvers were baby eels. So I
asked him what he thought they were, and he had a very good answer. 'If
you ask me,' he said, 'I'd say they were a miracle.'   5
    He was in good company. Even Izaac Walton after grave consideration
of the question came to the conclusion that they were bred 'either of dew or
out of the corruption of the earth'. His contemporaries held similar views,
that they were generated by the rays of the sun acting upon putrefying
matter, sprang from rotting seaweed or could be propagated artificially by   10
placing hairs from horses' tails in a stream. No man had at that time any
reason to suppose that the tiny wriggling things inhabiting our rivers in the
spring had already swum three thousand miles across the seas, and no man
had ever seen eel spawn or found an eel with eggs in her. These wild
guesses were no more improbable than the fantastic truth.   15
    The story of the eels' journey to their mating, and the elvers' journey
back, has always fascinated me, and I was once fortunate enough to witness
the very beginning of the journey. I was driving my car late one September
evening when the headlights picked out what looked like a water-splash
rippling across the road. I slowed down and saw that the foot-wide strip of   20
gleaming silver was not water, but was made up of a great company of eels,
wriggling in procession from one side of the road to the other.
    When I told the story to my wife, it was received with disbelief, but eels
they were all right, and the shining silver of their coats was the outward and
visible sign of their destiny. They were off to the Sargasso, and so they had   25
changed their yellowish-grey colour for the universal argent of the seas.
They had equipped themselves for the voyage in other ways too, and when
the adaptation was complete they had heard the ancient imperious call
which drew them willy-nilly toward the sea. There was no disobeying the
call, for it is death to disobey. If they had stayed, their skins, fitted out to   30
withstand the pressures below the surface of the sea, would have blistered
and burst. So they had wriggled through the mud until they reached the
painful obstacle of the highroad. Safely across it, they had water all the rest
of the way, and thereafter they would navigate themselves, as accurately as
any mariner equipped with compass, sextant or radar, across 3,000 miles of   35
ocean. Then they would mate, lay their eggs and die. No adult eel has ever
returned from that long journey.

    [13]

a) What was unusual about the man eating the elver cake?

....

b) Why does the writer say the man's answer was a good one?

....

c) What was the 'good company' the man was in?

....

d) Give two reasons that were suggested for the origin of elvers, one depending on human intervention and one not.

....

....

e) Explain the phrase 'sprang from' (line 10). ....

f) Explain in other words the phrase 'wild guesses' (line 14). ....

....

g) What did the author think he saw in the headlights of his car? ....

....

h) Why are the eels described as being 'in procession' (line 22)? ....

....

i) In what way was the colour of their coats 'the outward and visible sign of their destiny' (line 24)?

....

j) Explain the phrase 'willy-nilly' (line 29). ....

k) What was 'ancient' and 'imperious' (line 28) about the call the eels heard?

....

....

l) In what way was it death to disobey the call? (line 30)

....

m) Why was the highroad a 'painful obstacle'? (line 33) ....

....

[14]

n) What was surprising about the navigation of the eels? ....

....

o) Summarise in 50–100 words what the passage says about the life cycle of an eel from birth to death.

....

....

....

....

....

....

....

....

PAPER 4 LISTENING COMPREHENSION
(25 minutes)

FIRST PART

For questions 1–7, fill in the times on the notepad below (the first one has been filled in for you). For each of questions 8–10 put a tick ($\vee$) in one of the boxes A, B, C or D ($\boxed{A \vee}$ *etc.).*

Stratford Trip	Time
1. coach arrives	9.00
2. journey begins	___
3. arrive in Stratford	___
4. dinner is served	___
5. play begins	___
6. leave Stratford	___
7. get back at	___

8 Why shouldn't they be hungry on the way?

A Lunch has been booked in Stratford.

B Dinner has been booked in Stratford.

C They can eat on the bus.

D They can ask the bus to stop.

A
B
C
D

[16]

9 What might they have to pay for?

   A Dinner at the Bell Hotel.

   B Transport to the theatre.

   C Seats at the theatre.

   D Visit to Shakespeare's birthplace.

A
B
C
D

10 Why doesn't it matter if they don't understand everything in the play?

   A They will discuss it on the way back.

   B They will be able to enjoy half of it.

   C Many English people find Shakespeare difficult.

   D Many English people don't enjoy Shakespeare.

A
B
C
D

SECOND PART

For each of questions 11–15 put a tick in one of the boxes A, B, C or D.

11 Tom believes that the toy he is demonstrating is suitable for children because they

   A like playing with junk material.

   B like wiring up electric circuits.

   C don't like expensive toys.

   D don't need elaborate toys.

A
B
C
D

12 Tom says the toy is attractive to fathers because

   A it doesn't make a loud noise.

   B they can put it together easily.

   C it teaches a child to make electrical toys.

   D they can show off their skill as electricians.

A
B
C
D

13 What is the purpose of the toy's electric motor?

   A It makes an interesting noise.

   B It makes the toy spin round.

   C It lights up the bulbs.

   D It makes it more like a toy racing car.

A
B
C
D

[17]

14 In order to make the bulb grow brighter it is necessary to

   A speed up the engine.

   B attach it to the battery.

   C slow down the engine.

   D attach a series of wires to it.

A
B
C
D

15 Tom suggests the interviewer is not interested in the toy because

   A he hasn't any children.

   B he is too old.

   C he doesn't like toys.

   D he is too simple.

A
B
C
D

THIRD PART

For each of questions 16–19 put a tick in one of the boxes A, B, C or D.

16 The official speaks slowly and deliberately because he is

   A bored.

   B being reassuring.

   C annoyed.

   D being awkward.

A
B
C
D

17 The woman shows she is distressed by the way she

   A argues with the man.

   B objects to his questions.

   C repeats herself.

   D forgets her daughter's name.

A
B
C
D

18 What might the man be thinking when he learns the girl's name?

   A 'We've already traced her.'

   B 'I shall never manage to calm her.'

   C 'I don't believe this woman's story.'

   D 'Now I can get some details.'

A
B
C
D

[18]

19 At the end of the conversation the man has succeeded in

A upsetting her even further.

B removing her fears.

C extracting some information.

D finding the child.

A	
B	
C	
D	

FOURTH PART

For questions 20 and 21 look at the racing calendar, and for question 22 the list of jockeys on the right.

	Date	Race course	Country
1	October 1st	Salisbury	England
2		Longchamps	France
3		Kempton Park (annual team event part one)	England
4	October 24th	Belmont Park (annual team event part two)	

Carson	
Piggott	
Swinburne	
Starkey	
Mercer	
Eddery	

20 At which racing event, 1, 2, 3 or 4, is Starkey banned from riding?

....

21 Fill in the three spaces on the racing calendar above.

22 Look at the list of British jockeys. Tick the box beside those jockeys who are riding in the annual team event.

PAPER 5   INTERVIEW   (about 15 minutes)

SECTION A: PICTURE CONVERSATION

You will be asked to talk about one of the photographs among the Interview Exercises at the back of this book. Your teacher will tell you which one of the photographs to look at.

SECTION B: READING PASSAGE

You will be asked to read aloud one of the reading passages among the Interview Exercises at the back of this book. Your teacher will tell you which one of the reading passages to look at.

SECTION C: STRUCTURED COMMUNICATION ACTIVITY

You will be asked to take part in a conversation with a group of other students or with your teacher. Your teacher will tell you which section among the Interview Exercises you should look at.

Practice Test 2

PAPER 1   READING COMPREHENSION   (1 hour)

*This paper is in two parts, section A and section B. For each question you answer correctly in section A you gain **one** mark; for each question you answer correctly in section B you gain **two** marks. No marks are deducted for wrong answers. Answer all the questions. Indicate your choice of answer in every case on the separate sheet which should show your name and examination index number. Follow carefully the instructions about how to record your answer.*

SECTION A

In this section you must choose the word or phrase which best completes each sentence. For each question, 1 to 25, indicate on your answer sheet the letter A, B, C or D against the number of the question.

1 The main road through Salisbury was blocked for two hours today after an accident .... several vehicles.
   A containing   B connecting   C involving   D including

2 The company directors asked the government to .... in the dispute and prevent a strike.
   A intervene   B interact   C intercept   D interpose

3 After the campaign a special medal was .... to all combatants.
   A gained   B awarded   C earned   D deserved

4 The usual reason for exemption from tax does not .... in this case.
   A apply   B impose   C regard   D concern

5 We don't sell foreign newspapers because there is no .... for them.
   A request   B claim   C requirement   D demand

6 In the legal profession, men .... women by five to one.
   A outnumber   B supersede   C overcome   D outclass

7 At the last concert we had the privilege of .... the composer's latest symphony.
   A listening   B attending   C assisting   D hearing

⟫→

[21]

8 I must take this watch to be repaired; it .... over twenty minutes a day.
   A increases   B progresses   C accelerates   D gains

9 Luckily my wallet was handed in to the police with all its contents ....
   A preserved   B unscathed   C contained   D intact

10 A minority of the committee members were dissatisfied with the decision and endeavoured to .... it.
    A overturn   B abolish   C postpone   D re-do

11 If this animal had escaped from its cage it could .... have killed or maimed several people.
    A equally   B both   C well   D severely

12 Time was running out, so the committee had to make a .... decision.
    A brief   B snap   C sharp   D curt

13 Because of an unfortunate .... your order was not despatched by the date requested.
    A hindrance   B oversight   C negligence   D transgression

14 Motorists .... of speeding may be banned from driving for a year.
    A convicted   B arrested   C charged   D judged

15 If you walk along this lane you will see the signpost .... to the beach.
    A pointing   B showing   C directing   D indicating

16 She didn't .... doing the ironing, as she hadn't wanted to go out anyway.
    A object   B matter   C care for   D mind

17 The decision was .... to a later meeting.
    A cancelled   B arranged   C deferred   D delayed

18 Tempers began to .... as the lorries forced their way through the picket lines.
    A break   B fray   C grate   D fire

19 The old ship will be towed into harbour and ....
    A broken up   B broken down   C broken in   D broken off

20 Making private calls on the office phone is severely .... on in our department.
    A frowned   B criticised   C regarded   D objected

21 The tank of petrol was .... by a carelessly discarded cigarette end.
   A lit up   B ignited   C exploded   D inflamed

22 The government has made no .... in the fight against inflation; indeed,
the situation has worsened recently.
   A headway   B effect   C avail   D triumph

23 They managed to free him from the burning car in the .... of time
before the tank exploded.
   A tick   B wink   C nick   D brink

24 I'm sorry we gave you such short .... of our visit.
   A caution   B notice   C information   D preparation

25 He was so mean that he couldn't bear to .... the smallest sum of money
for the charity appeal.
   A pay off   B part with   C give in   D let out

SECTION B

In this section you will find after each of the passages a number of questions or unfinished statements about the passage, each with four suggested answers or ways of finishing. You must choose the one which you think fits best. For each question, 26 to 40, indicate on your answer sheet the letter A, B, C or D against the number of the question.

FIRST PASSAGE

April the 3rd was the day we attempted to reach Mount Everest. The morning saw us all up and rushing about the bungalow at daybreak. We bumped down the nine miles of dusty track, each clutching a camera or one of the more delicate instruments to our chests in an endeavour to make our bodies absorb as many of the shocks from the bumpy track as possible. The ground staff were already busy on our arrival. The sheds where the aircraft were kept had been opened and the great machines were being manhandled out onto the tarmac. The bottles of oxygen were carefully placed in their clips and connected to the system. The vertical cameras were fitted and tested, air frames and engines were inspected and tested in every detail.

    Pilots and observers fussed around their equipment, trying on oxygen masks which they had tried on many times before, re-adjusting straps, electric leads and oxygen feed pipes that had already been adjusted to a nicety. They then re-checked the charts which had been carefully prepared to allow accurately for the increasing wind speeds during the climb – all trying to keep themselves occupied during that tense half-hour wait for the return of the reconnaissance machine.

    There had been so much preparation for this flight, and there was still so much of the unknown about it, that the crews could not help being slightly affected by the general excitement. Waiting is always unpleasant, and we were all relieved to see the reconnaissance machine diving down through the dust haze. The Air Commodore who commanded it brought welcome news. Though he had been unable to climb above the dust, he had been able to see towards the mountains through the top of the haze and there was a cloudless sky. This was splendid: no cloud to mar the photography.

We had promised not to attempt the flight if the wind exceeded 40 miles an hour, but this was the first time we had found the wind under 100 miles an hour. We worked out the implications and reckoned that, provided we did not spend more than fifteen minutes at the summit, we could get back inside our petrol endurance. We might wait for days and weeks and not get another opportunity. The Air Commodore weighed the position carefully and gave the word 'Go'.

26   The author and his colleagues held their instruments close to their bodies
     because
     A   there were so many people in the car.
     B   the dust might have obscured their cameras.
     C   the surface of the track was very uneven.
     D   they wanted to protect themselves from bumps.

27   When the members of the expedition arrived at the aerodrome, the ground
     staff were
     A   manoeuvring the aircraft into position on the runway.
     B   attaching the clips to the bottles of oxygen.
     C   waiting to remove the machines from the sheds.
     D   making final adjustments to the vertical cameras.

28   The crews of the aircraft kept checking their equipment
     A   to ensure that the straps on their oxygen masks were adjustable.
     B   to pinpoint the position of the reconnaissance plane.
     C   to verify the accuracy of the wind speeds shown in their charts.
     D   to keep themselves busy until it was time to take off.

29   For this expedition the pilots were equipped with
     A   a television system.
     B   a new type of aircraft.
     C   breathing apparatus.
     D   parachute equipment.

30   During the reconnaissance flight the Air Commodore was able to
     A   get close to the summit of Mount Everest.
     B   observe the weather conditions above the dust.
     C   take long-range photographs of the mountain.
     D   send information back to the aerodrome.

31 The purpose of this expedition to Mount Everest was to
    A investigate the atmospheric conditions on the mountain.
    B make an aerial survey of the summit.
    C test the breathing apparatus at high altitude.
    D penetrate the dust haze surrounding the mountain.

SECOND PASSAGE

Standing alone at the Browns' party, Anna Mackintosh thought about her husband Edward, establishing him clearly in her mind's eye. He was a thin man, forty-one years of age, with fair hair that was often untidy. In the seventeen years they'd been married he had changed very little: he was still nervous with other people, and smiled in the same abashed way, and his face was still almost boyish.

She believed she had failed him because he had wished for children and she had not been able to supply any. She had, over the years, become neurotic about this fact and in the end, quite some time ago now, she had consulted a psychiatrist, a Dr Abbat, at Edward's pleading.

In the Browns' rich drawing room, its walls and ceiling gleaming with a metallic surface of imitation gold, Anna listened to dance music coming from a tape recorder and continued to think about her husband.

In a moment he would be at the party too, since they had agreed to meet there, although by now it was three-quarters of an hour later than the time he had stipulated.

The Browns were people he knew in a business way, and he had said he thought it wise that he and Anna should attend this gathering of theirs. She had never met them before, which made it more difficult for her, having to wait about, not knowing a soul in the room.

When she thought about it she felt hard done by, for although Edward was kind to her and always had been, it was far from considerate to be as late as this. Because of her nervous condition she felt afraid and had developed a sickness in her stomach. She looked at her watch and sighed.

32 Why does Anna feel awkward at the party?
    A Her husband's nervousness affects her.
    B She doesn't like the Browns.
    C Her husband isn't coming.
    D She doesn't know anybody.

33 What makes Anna feel inadequate?
    A Her bad relationship with her husband.
    B Her husband's youthful appearance.
    C Her inability to have children.
    D Her lack of success at parties.

⟫⟶

34   Anna starts to get angry because
    A   she resents the Browns' wealth.
    B   she isn't feeling very well.
    C   her husband is usually more thoughtful.
    D   the Browns are only business acquaintances.

35   Why did Edward want Anna to attend the party?
    A   He was going to be late.
    B   He wanted her to have more of a social life.
    C   He needed her support.
    D   He thought she would impress the Browns.

THIRD PASSAGE

If we join the Pembrokeshire Coast Path at the Cardigan end we start by climbing steadily up a narrow road, past the youth hostel, for a mile or so, till we reach a farm.

As we continue to climb, the view down to the right, across the mouth of the river towards Cardigan Island, becomes more and more impressive. When we have climbed to nearly 400 feet we see a steep drop to the rocks and sea below. Look back at the amazing folds in the cliff face caused by earth movements some 400 million years ago.

We continue to climb up to more than 550 feet above the waves breaking below. The path, narrow and uncomfortably close to the edge at times, now broadens out where a small earth-mover with a five-foot blade was used. Spare a thought for the courage of the man who drove it, whether or not you like the result.

Coming down from this highest point of the whole coastal footpath we pass through rough grass and a rich variety of wild flowers. The variety depends on what time of year we are walking, but many will be flowering even in mid-winter. Please leave them to do so.

We arrive at sea level, among the rock pools which tempt us to pause for a while. From here we follow the bank of a stream uphill; (it needs care not to slide into it). Down to our right is a platform, where thoughtless people have seen fit to pile up their unwanted cars.

We descend through a rather muddy field to a picnic area where we may very possibly see another human being for the first time in more than two hours' walking. The next four miles or so remain chiefly in the memory for the steepness of the path in places. With several steep ups and downs the general direction is upwards till we are on Morfa Head. Below we can see caves in the cliff and a natural arch of rocks. This is a view to enjoy for a few minutes before plunging down the grassy slope to the north end of Newport Sands.

[26]

36 In this passage the writer is addressing
    A experienced mountaineers.
    B any interested individuals.
    C students of geography.
    D plant collectors.

37 The language of the passage could be described as
    A witty.
    B technical.
    C conversational.
    D formal.

38 The writer occasionally addresses the reader directly in order to
    A encourage him to continue.
    B warn him of dangers.
    C make him think.
    D reprimand him.

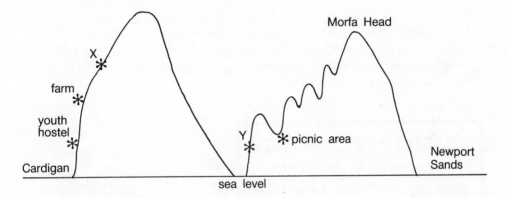

39 From the point marked X on the cross-section it is possible to see
    A abandoned cars.
    B caves in the cliff.
    C a natural arch of rocks.
    D Cardigan Island.

40 At the point marked Y on the cross-section the writer hopes the reader will
    A take care.
    B walk faster.
    C look at the flowers.
    D meet another walker.

PAPER 2 COMPOSITION (2 hours)

*Write **two only** of the following composition exercises. Your answers must follow exactly the instructions given. Write in pen, not pencil. You are allowed to make alterations, but see that your work is clear and easy to read.*

1 Describe the career you have chosen, and the reasons for your choice. (About 350 words)

2 What should be done to preserve world peace? (About 350 words)

3 A ghost story that could be true. (About 200 words)

4 You applied for the post in the following advertisement, and were delighted to be offered the job. The headlines below refer to events which took place at the school about a month after you took up the post. Write, in about 200 words, a letter to a friend, expressing your feelings about what happened and seeking help in your predicament.

TEACH YOUR LANGUAGE

to small groups of English students at the Modern Language Centre, Oxbridge, beginning January 1984. Monthly salary, board and lodging at the Centre. Excellent facilities and teaching conditions. Annual return air ticket. Experience unnecessary, orientation provided. Applicants must be over 21 years of age and university graduates.

5th Feb.
LANGUAGE SCHOOL BOSS REJECTS CHARGE
Facilities 'Second to None'

4th Feb.
LANGUAGE SCHOOL FRAUD
Non-existent Lang. Lab., Video pictured in Prospectus
'NOT WHAT WE PAID FOR' CLAIM UPSET STUDENTS

8th Feb.
Hygiene Risk School Kitchens Closed Down

12th Feb.
STRANDED SCHOOL STAFF SEEK REDRESS

11th Feb.
Disquiet over Staff Work Permits at troubled School
LABOUR WITHDRAWAL THREAT

15th Feb
MLC: Director absconds with Funds

5 Basing your answer on your reading of the prescribed text concerned, answer *one* of the following. (About 350 words)

SHAKESPEARE: *Hamlet*
How much of the human motivation in this play seems to have any recognisable force today?

HARDY: *Far From the Madding Crowd*
What do you find interesting, as a non-English person of the twentieth century, in the social structure of Hardy's world?

KATHERINE MANSFIELD: *The Garden Party and Other Stories*
Katherine Mansfield has been praised in recent years as an important figure in women's writing. What do you think is meant by this, and what is your opinion?

PAPER 3   USE OF ENGLISH   (2 hours)

SECTION A

1   *Fill each of the numbered blanks in the following passage with* **one** *suitable word.*

Many people persuade themselves that they cannot understand mechanical things, or that they have no head for figures. These convictions .... (1) them feel enclosed and safe, and .... (2) course save them a great .... (3) of trouble. But the reader who has a head for anything at .... (4) is pretty sure to have a head for whatever he really wants to put his mind .... (5). His interest, say .... (6) mathematics, has usually been killed .... (7) routine teaching, in exactly the .... (8) way that the literary interest of most scientists, and for .... (9) matter of most non-scientists, has been killed by the set book and the Shakespeare play. Few people would argue that .... (10) whose taste .... (11) poetry has not survived .... (12) examination syllabus are fundamentally insensitive .... (13) poetry. Yet they cheerfully write .... (14) the large intellectual pleasures of science .... (15) if they belonged only to minds .... (16) a special cast. Science is not a special sense. It is as wide as the literal meaning .... (17) its name: knowledge. The notion of the specialised mind is, ... (18) comparison, ... (19) modern as the notion of the specialised man, 'the scientist', a word which is only .... (20) hundred years old.

2   *Finish each of the following sentences in such a way that it means exactly the same as the sentence printed before it.*

EXAMPLE: Immediately after his arrival, things went wrong.

ANSWER: No sooner *had he arrived than things went wrong.*

[30]

a) If you want my advice, I would forget about buying a new house.

    If I ....

b) 'I don't love you any more,' said Eric to his girlfriend.

    Eric told his girlfriend that ....

c) 'I must see the manager!' he cried.

    He insisted ....

d) Arthur said he was sorry he had hurt her feelings.

    Arthur apologised ....

e) I had better get back to work.

    It's ....

f) The last time it rained was a fortnight ago.

    It ....

g) The noise next door did not stop until after midnight.

    It was not ....

h) The car was so rusty that it couldn't be repaired.

    The car was too ....

i) He never has enough money.

    He's always ....

j) Yogurt is supposed to be good for you.

    Yogurt is supposed to do ....

3   *Fill each of the blanks with a suitable word or phrase.*

      EXAMPLE: Even if I had stood on a chair, *I wouldn't have been able to*
             reach the light bulb.

a) The children were .... to their holiday.

b) His cold attitude showed that he was not .... being criticised.

c) I wish .... met him.

d) If only her father .... agree I could marry her now.

e) I'll lend you the money as .... you promise to give it back.

f) Don't .... iron that shirt; it's a waste of time.

g) It might take him six months to .... his illness.

h) How long .... with your left hand?
Ever since I broke my right arm.

i) You'll have to work hard to .... with the rest of the class.

j) I'd make you some tea but we seem to have .... of milk.

4 *For each of the sentences below, write a new sentence as similar as possible in meaning to the original sentence, but using the words given in bold letters. The words must **not be altered** in any way.*

    EXAMPLE: His arrival was completely unexpected.
           took

    ANSWER: *His arrival took us completely by surprise.*

a) Sarah wore dark glasses so that no one would recognise her.
avoid

....

b) Anne was afraid the neighbours would despise her for not having a washing machine.
look

....

c) If only you had tried harder you might have passed the exam.
effort

....

d) 'I wonder if you could possibly open the door for me?'
mind

....

e) It might be better if that paragraph was omitted.
leave

....

f) Bill reckoned that his success was due to incredible luck.
put

....

g) Why not tell him the truth and be finished with it?
get

....

h) Martin had difficulty in accepting the loss of his money.
hard

....

i) It wasn't my intention to upset you.
mean

....

j) The children pestered us for sweets.
kept

....

SECTION B

5 *Read the following passage, then answer the questions which follow it, basing your answers entirely on the information given in the passage.*

With luck, we will all live to grow old, some of us very old indeed. What then are the pitfalls of age? One, ironically, is the product of affluence. More than half of the middle-aged who own their own houses have a fatal predilection for selling up on retirement and buying a dream home by the sea, drawn back by memories of sunlit holidays, forgetful of what bracing   5
sea air does to old bones (and heating bills).
    For the next 10 or 15 years the couple will live happily enough until one of them dies and the upkeep of the house, the garden and the running repairs become too much for the other on her own; 'her' because it is usually the husband who dies. Seaside towns do not have the resources or   10
the social services of big cities; relatives and old friends are far away. The house starts to crumble around her – literally. A lucky widow will then be

offered a flat by the social services, on one of these housing estates for the
old, but there is no way that a small seaside town can house all the sad old
women in need of help.   15

Old couples who decide against the move to the towns around Britain's
coastline may miss the dream cottage years of early retirement but they also
miss out on the subsequent distress. Because most of today's pensioners
were the children of large families, they probably have around 15 close
women relatives still alive, with a reasonable chance that one out of that 15   20
will be able and/or willing to care for them. Tomorrow's old are going to be
the children of much smaller families; they will be lucky to have five
relatives alive when they need help.

Very old people do, in fact, raise moral problems for almost everyone
who comes into contact with them. Their values – this can't be repeated too   25
often – are not necessarily our values. Physical comfort, cleanness, order
and discipline are not necessarily priorities. The social services from time to
time find themselves faced with a house crawling with rotten food, the food
crawling with maggots, and an old person contemplating both with
equanimity. Is it interfering with personal freedom to insist they go into a   30
home? Some social workers, the ones who clear up the maggots, think we
are in danger of carrying this concept of personal freedom to the point
where serious risks are being taken with the health and safety of the old.

Indeed, the old are vulnerable. Old age is not a disease, but minor,
untreated complaints can produce a very sick old person. The body is like a   35
car: it needs more mechanical tinkering as it gets older. You can carry this
analogy right through to the provision of spare parts. But never forget that
such operations involve major surgery and are painful ordeals, however
good the results. And at what point should you cease to treat the old body?
Is it morally right to try to push off death by pursuing the development of   40
drugs to stimulate the forgetful old mind and spare parts to rejuvenate the
old body, knowing that it is designed to die? You cannot ask doctors or
scientists to decide, because so long as they can see the technical
opportunities they will feel bound to give them a try, on the principle that
while there's life, there's hope.   45

When you talk to old people, however, you are forced to the conclusion
that whether age is happy or hellish depends less on money or on health
than it does on your own inner resources and on your ability to have fun.
The old-age lobbies which play so powerfully on our consciences have
made us feel, somehow, that it's our fault. It isn't.   50

a)   What is ironical about the problem discussed in the first paragraph?

....

....

....

[34]

b) Explain the phrase 'a fatal predilection' (lines 3–4). ....

....

c) What disadvantages does living by the sea have, according to the first paragraph?

....

....

d) What are 'running repairs' (lines 8–9)? ....

....

e) Explain the writer's use in line 12 of the word 'literally'. ....

....

f) Why are the old women described as 'sad' in line 14? ....

....

g) Why is it really better for pensioners to remain in their home areas on retirement?

....

....

....

h) Why does the writer insert the phrase 'this can't be repeated too often' (line 25)?

....

....

i) What example is given of the conflict in values that can arise? ....

....

j) In what ways, it is suggested here, is the human body like a motor car? ...

....

k) What is the meaning of 'rejuvenate' (line 41)? ....

....

l) Why, according to the writer, should medical decisions on the very old not be made by doctors alone?

....

....

m) What does the word 'it' in the last line refer to?   ....

n) How does the writer justify the conclusion that it isn't our fault?   ....

....

....

o) Summarise, in a paragraph of 50–100 words, what is said in the passage about the difficulties encountered by those people whose job it is to care for the old.

....

....

....

....

....

....

....

....

PAPER 4 LISTENING COMPREHENSION
(32 minutes)

FIRST PART

For questions 1–7 tick (√) which you think is the best answer in each case – A, B, C or D.

1 The first woman speaker complains about

    A multi-track stereo in a neighbouring house.

    B drivers accelerating on bends.

    C very loud music coming from the street.

    D people walking around with radios.

A
B
C
D

2 Last Sunday afternoon the interviewer

    A was almost deafened by noise.

    B made a lot of noise in her garden.

    C was attacked by barking dogs.

    D was alarmed by burglars.

A
B
C
D

3 Richard McRorey is

    A a diarist.

    B a DIY expert.

    C a doctor.

    D a lecturer.

A
B
C
D

4 What power does the environmental health officer have?

    A He can only act as an adviser.

    B He can evict your neighbours.

    C He can take your neighbours' dog away from them.

    D He can tell your neighbours to keep their dogs quiet.

A
B
C
D

[37]

5 Mr McRorey thinks that you should

   A note when unpleasant noises occur.

   B buy a huge dog.

   C treat neighbours as they treat you.

   D not forgive your neighbour.

A
B
C
D

6 Environmental health officers are employed by

   A the National Health Service.

   B night security firms.

   C local government.

   D the police.

A
B
C
D

7 This programme is intended to give useful advice about

   A home improvements.

   B citizens' rights.

   C motorcycle maintenance.

   D health services.

A
B
C
D

SECOND PART

For questions 8–12, tick (√) which you think is the best answer in each case – A, B, C or D.

8 What is the origin of the expression 'Mayday'?

   A It was first used on 1st May.

   B It sounds like the French words for 'help me'.

   C It was used during the First World War.

   D It was suggested by Mr Mockford's young son.

A
B
C
D

9 What was Mr Mockford's work in World War I?

   A He was a brain specialist.

   B He was a pilot at Hounslow.

   C He specialised in wireless telegraphy.

   D He was the Air Minister.

A
B
C
D

10 Why did the pilots have to contact Croydon Airport?

    A   To find out their location.

    B   To get a weather forecast.

    C   To speak to Pulham and Lympne.

    D   To check the exact time.

A
B
C
D

11 Why was the air-radio system unsatisfactory at first?

    A   It was considered an irrelevant novelty.

    B   Radios created extra weight.

    C   It was too expensive.

    D   Radios were often faulty.

A
B
C
D

12 Mockford's contribution to air safety

    A   is not well-known.

    B   appears in standard reference books.

    C   was well publicised during the war.

    D   is widely recognised.

A
B
C
D

THIRD PART

You are keen on sport. Your friend is keen on live music. Tick the box in each column opposite the place you or your friend might visit today.

	You (sport)	Your friend (music)
13 Horseguards		
14 Crystal Palace National Sports Centre		
15 St John's Wood		

⟫→

	You (sport)	*Your friend (music)*
16 Cumberland Hotel		
17 Crystal Palace Football Ground		
18 Holland Park		
19 Hyde Park		
20 Round House		
21 Queen Elizabeth Hall		
22 Crystal Palace Concert Bowl		

FOURTH PART

For questions 23–28 tick (√) whether you think the statements are True or False.

	True	False
23 At first, Mr Peters was nervous when he was talking to the policeman.		
24 Mr Peters freely admitted driving to Westwater during the afternoon of the 7th April.		
25 Mr Peters refused to tell the policeman when he was between Whitebridge and the roundabout.		
26 Mr Peters wanted to know why he was being questioned.		
27 When Mr Peters said, 'I'm aware of that,' he feared he was going to be accused of dangerous driving.		
28 When Mr Peters said, 'Oh, you mean, did I witness anything?', he sounded quite angry.		

PAPER 5   INTERVIEW   (about 15 minutes)

SECTION A: PICTURE CONVERSATION

You will be asked to talk about one of the photographs among the Interview Exercises at the back of this book. Your teacher will tell you which one of the photographs to look at.

SECTION B: READING PASSAGE

You will be asked to read aloud one of the reading passages among the Interview Exercises at the back of this book. Your teacher will tell you which one of the reading passages to look at.

SECTION C: STRUCTURED COMMUNICATION ACTIVITY

You will be asked to take part in a conversation with a group of other students or with your teacher. Your teacher will tell you which section among the Interview Exercises you should look at.

Practice Test 3

PAPER 1   READING COMPREHENSION   (1 hour)

This paper is in two parts, section A and section B. For each question you answer correctly in section A you gain **one** *mark; for each question you answer correctly in section B you gain* **two** *marks. No marks are deducted for wrong answers. Answer all the questions. Indicate your choice of answer in every case on the separate sheet which should show your name and examination index number. Follow carefully the instructions about how to record your answer.*

SECTION A

In this section you must choose the word or phrase which best completes each sentence. For each question, 1 to 25, indicate on your answer sheet the letter A, B, C or D against the number of the question.

1   That old vase will .... an attractive lamp-holder.
    A compose   B form   C make   D assemble

2   After a long and exhausting journey, they arrived home ....
    A finally   B by the end   C at the end   D at last

3   I cannot bear the noise of my brother's radio; it .... me from my work.
    A disturbs   B perturbs   C interrupts   D distracts

4   The World Bank has criticised Britain for not giving enough financial .... to developing countries.
    A allowance   B aid   C loan   D provision

5   After a short holiday, he .... himself once more to his studies.
    A applied   B converted   C engaged   D exerted

6   By the age of twenty-five he had .... his ambition of becoming a pianist.
    A reached   B completed   C achieved   D obtained

7   There is .... to be a serious energy crisis in the next century.
    A reputed   B known   C bound   D foreseen

8   It had been a trying afternoon, ... at about six o'clock in the television breaking down.
    A leading   B culminating   C arriving   D finalising

⟫⟫→

[43]

9 The completion of the new Town Hall has been .... owing to a strike.
   A held off   B held down   C held up   D held on

10 I was .... by the wording of the advertisement.
   A mistaken   B misled   C misunderstood   D misguided

11 Although they are identical twins their teacher can easily .... between them.
   A identify   B differ   C select   D distinguish

12 Dr Smith uses student volunteers as .... for his experiments.
   A subjects   B models   C cases   D agents

13 Not knowing he had .... out with his girlfriend, I made the mistake of inviting them both to the party.
   A fallen   B quarrelled   C parted   D separated

14 He showed his .... for the TV programme by switching it off.
   A distaste   B discontent   C annoyance   D boredom

15 People under 21 years old are not .... to join this club.
   A desirable   B eligible   C advisable   D admissible

16 Because the law moves so slowly, there is a considerable .... of untried cases.
   A hangover   B remainder   C backlog   D reserve

17 News of the attempted coup began to .... through to the outside world.
   A pour   B filter   C broadcast   D drip

18 John's in hospital again. The poor chap seems .... to accidents.
   A prone   B disposed   C bound   D destined

19 'I know that you have an appointment in ten minutes, so I shall not .... you long,' the professor remarked.
   A retard   B withhold   C postpone   D detain

20 He was awarded the medal for 'displaying professional competence of the highest .... in the rescue attempts.'
   A ability   B order   C position   D credit

21 He gave me a furious look and .... out of the room.
   A stormed   B hurled   C surged   D burst

22 'My secretary was .... to have typed those letters already.'
   A asked   B supposed   C requested   D ordered

23 He seems very quiet, but it would be a mistake to .... his intelligence.
    A devalue   B depreciate   C underrate   D minimise

24 I am well .... with the problems encountered in starting a business.
    A aware   B informed   C acquainted   D knowledgeable

25 If production in that factory exceeds the target, the workers get a ....
    A bonus   B gratuity   C donation   D subsidy

SECTION B

In this section you will find after each of the passages a number of questions or unfinished statements about the passage, each with four suggested answers or ways of finishing. You must choose the one which you think fits best. For each question, 26 to 40, indicate on your answer sheet the letter A, B, C or D against the number of the question.

FIRST PASSAGE

Whatever may be said against mass circulation magazines and newspapers, it can hardly be argued that they are out of touch with their readers' daydreams, and therefore the inducements they hold out to them must be a near accurate reflection of their unfulfilled wants and aspirations. Study these and you will assuredly understand a good deal of what it is that makes society tick.

Looking back, for example, to the twenties and thirties, we can see that circulation managers unerringly diagnosed the twin obsessions which dominated that era of mass unemployment – economic insecurity and a passionate concern for the next generation. Thus it was that readers were recruited with offers of free insurance policies for the one, and free instant education for the other. The family whose breadwinner lost an eye in a double railway derailment, or an arm in a flood, could confidently expect to collect several hundred pounds from the Daily This or the Evening That. The family who could not afford to send their son to grammar school could find consolation in equipping him with the complete works of Shakespeare in one magnificent, easy to read volume.

After the war the need to fall into step with the new consumer society was soon realised. If you were flanked by neighbours who, unlike you, could afford a holiday abroad, then winning an easy competition could set you up with a fortnight in an exotic sunspot. Dishwashers, washing machines, slow-cookers and deep-fat-friers were – and still are – available by the same means.

26 The writer finds the study of gifts and prizes interesting because it
    A   shows the power of the popular press.
    B   reveals social trends.
    C   confirms his view of human nature.
    D   exposes journalistic dishonesty.

⟫→

[45]

27 Why did newspapers in the 1920s and 1930s offer their readers gifts?
   A   To spread popular education.
   B   To increase their circulation.
   C   To improve social conditions.
   D   To increase their readers' ambitions.

28 What does the choice of gifts tell us about the circulation managers?
   A   They despised their readers.
   B   Their interests were rather serious.
   C   They understood their readers.
   D   They enjoyed being powerful.

29 Why were readers in the 1920s and 1930s attracted by free insurance policies?
   A   They were afraid of being unable to work.
   B   Jobs were more dangerous then.
   C   They had bigger families to look after.
   D   Money was given away with the policies.

30 Why were books a popular gift?
   A   The books could be passed on to the next generation.
   B   The books were special editions for children.
   C   Parents could save money on school expenses.
   D   People wanted to do their best for their children.

31 Why did holidays abroad become a common prize after the war?
   A   People became more interested in material possessions.
   B   Everyone wanted the opportunity to travel.
   C   Group travel became easier.
   D   People wanted to get away from familiar surroundings.

SECOND PASSAGE

Seeing the wreck for the first time, under the great arc of a sunny sky on that level shore, I was initially struck by its remoteness. Here was the focus of those weeks of discussion, of seemingly endless careful planning: a slightly projecting, elongated outline.

The warmth of the day meant that many holidaymakers were about, and our equipment rapidly attracted them to the site, unmistakeable with its brilliant orange markers, each attached to a steel post. These posts marked off the four corners of our working area, and were linked by a rope to keep it clear of curious sightseers.

Many structural features of the wreck which would normally have been visible were obscured by the sand, which was not only right up to but even above the upper gun deck. We went to work immediately the first low tide made a start possible, and set up our basic survey line running down the middle of the wreck from bow to stern. As we set about measuring the sides of the ship in their relation to the survey line, the 'Amsterdam' emerged as a vessel of substance, and more so when the members of the team had scoured her aged timbers free from mussel shells and seaweed.

All this activity attracted an increasing number of sightseers, whose interest was natural and welcome, since the more people who were moved to understand what we were about, the better it was for archaeology in general and for the future preservation of the 'Amsterdam' in particular. However, there were also predatory souvenir hunters who were most disappointed by our merely taking elaborate measurements, with no apparent intention of digging up more objects.

32 When he first saw the wreck of the 'Amsterdam' the author was impressed
    by
    A   its accessibility from the shore.
    B   the crowds of people round it.
    C   the effect of its outline against the sky.
    D   its apparent isolation.

33 The holidaymakers on the beach were
    A   confined within a roped-off area.
    B   discouraged from entering a roped-off area.
    C   confined to the upper part of the wreck.
    D   kept well away from the orange markers.

34 Work on the wreck was made difficult by
    A   the slope of the beach.
    B   the height of the ship.
    C   the position of the sand.
    D   the strength of the tide.

35 The 'Amsterdam' had been
    A   a submarine.
    B   a warship.
    C   a passenger liner.
    D   a fishing boat.

THIRD PASSAGE

Questions 36 to 40 refer to the following letters.

A

Myth of road needs exploding

Sir,
The myth of an 'Inner Relief Road or nothing' needs exploding once and for all. Repeatedly we are threatened that if we do not accept the Inner Relief Road we will get nothing, and our M.P. last week hinted at 10 years of increasing chaos if it is not built.

What kind of logic says that if one remedy is unacceptable, another will not be tried? Surely even if another scheme in the county takes precedence over the one for Ripon, it does not mean that Ripon has to go to the bottom of the list.

R.W.E.

B

Knowing where we stand

Sir,
The Outer Bypass Group wrote to our M.P. seeking his opinion on the Relief Road issue. At the public meeting I read out his reply, in which he stated that his sympathies had always been with an outer bypass provided a suitable route could be found.

K.F.

C

M.P. on road issue

Sir,
Mr Spence has once again referred to my ignorance of the issues in the roads dispute. I fear he is striving to hide his own embarrassment, having switched sides on the issue.

Let me say it yet again: an outer bypass used to be my preferred option, and I believe that County officials would also prefer such a solution if the arithmetic added up. But what is the point of a good idea if it has not a cat in hell's chance of becoming reality? That 'bit longer' which people keep talking about might be very long indeed, with everyone's environment deteriorating under the impact of heavy lorries, to say nothing of serious damage to the Cathedral.

K.H.
House of Commons, London

D

Effect of inner road

Sir,
What will happen to our town if an inner relief road is built? It will be cut in half. The oldest buildings will be torn down, rooted out, because they stand on the proposed route. The west side of the city will be amputated from the body of the town.

The schools, the hospital and the parks will be separated from the whole town and only reachable by risking life and limb crossing the main arterial road.

The life of the city will become more and more feeble till it eventually dies.

Please save our city!

Mother of Five

36   In which letter does the writer express the warmest feelings for Ripon?

37   In which letter has the writer had a change of heart?

38   In which letter does the writer think that further ideas should be explored?

39   Which letter is concerned about a place of worship?

40   In which letter does the writer use expressions from medical terminology?

PAPER 2 COMPOSITION (2 hours)

*Write **two only** of the following composition exercises. Your answers must follow exactly the instructions given. Write in pen, not pencil. You are allowed to make alterations, but see that your work is clear and easy to read.*

1 Describe *either* your best friend *or* your worst enemy. (About 350 words)

2 'I never smack my child.' Do you think this kind of parent is right? (About 350 words)

3 An experience that taught you the usefulness of learning a foreign language. (About 200 words)

4 The following is an advertisement of a house for sale in a British newspaper. A friend is looking for a house in this particular district. Write all the relevant information about the house in one paragraph of about 200 words as you would include it in a letter to him. (Do not write the rest of the letter.)

> **FASHIONABLE N.W.1** By Camden Sq.
> Film producer has lovingly reconstr. this
> impressive early Vict. family hse. Gas
> cent. heat. Elegant 30ft Drawing Rm.
> Dining Rm. parquet, drs. to 50ft gdn., 4
> bedrms. (2 dble), all fit wdrbs., fully fit
> kit/b'fast rm., dble sinks. FHLD ONLY
> £119,000. View Sun 01-233 0541.

5 Basing your answer on your reading of the prescribed text concerned, answer *one* of the following. (About 350 words)

DICKENS: *David Copperfield*
Describe some ways in which Dickens gives an especially strong and immediate feeling of life in a vanished era.

D. H. LAWRENCE: *Sons and Lovers*
What do you think is the most important relationship in this book?

SAUL BELLOW: *Henderson the Rain King*
What lessons about the values of life do you think the author is seeking to express?

PAPER 3   USE OF ENGLISH   (2 hours)

SECTION A

1   *Fill each of the numbered blanks in the following passage with* **one** *suitable word.*

British television is the big success story of post-war years. Little
.... (1) than a limited experiment before the war, it blossomed in
.... (2) years following 1945. .... (3) 1955, commercial
television began. Today, 90 per cent of the population have television in
.... (4) homes.

In 1960, a committee of enquiry was .... (5) up,
.... (6) the chairmanship of Sir Harry Pilkington, to investigate the
workings of broadcasting. The Pilkington Report, published in 1962, had
.... (7) to say:

'Television has been .... (8) a mirror of society, but the
metaphor, ... (9) striking, wholly misses the major issue of the
responsibility .... (10) the broadcasting authorities. For, if we
consider the first aspect of this responsibility, what is the .... (11)
to reflect? Is it to reflect the best or the worst .... (12) us? One cannot
escape the question by saying that it must do both; one must ask then
.... (13) it is to present the best and the worst with complete
indifference and .... (14) comment. Television .... (15)
not, and cannot, merely reflect the moral standards of society. It must affect
.... (16) either by changing or by reinforcing them.'

All broadcasting, and television .... (17), must be ready and
anxious to experiment, to show .... (18) new and unusual, to give a
hearing .... (19) dissent. Here, broadcasting must be most willing
to make mistakes; for if it does not, it will .... (20) no discoveries.

2 *Finish each of the following sentences in such a way that it means exactly the same as the sentence printed before it.*

EXAMPLE: Immediately after his arrival, things went wrong.

ANSWER: No sooner *had he arrived than things went wrong.*

a) Although the play received good notices, not many people went to see it.

Despite ....

b) My father speaks very little English.

My father speaks hardly ....

c) He said he was not guilty of stealing the car.

He denied ....

d) I'm sorry now that I asked her to stay.

Now I wish ....

e) They couldn't trace who had supplied the information in the first place.

The source ....

f) There is always trouble when he comes to visit us.

Whenever ....

g) Is this the only way to reach the city centre?

Isn't there ....?

h) He never suspected that the money had been stolen.

At no time ....

i) I have never seen such a mess in my life!

Never in ....

j) Is it essential to meet your aunt at the station?

Does your aunt ....?

3 *Fill each of the blanks with a suitable word or phrase.*

    EXAMPLE: Even if I had stood on a chair, *I wouldn't have been able to* reach the light bulb.

a) 'I've got a dreadful headache.'

    'You'd .... go to bed for a while.'

b) 'I first met John in 1964.'

    'Goodness! You .... for a very long time, then.'

c) This bottle is nearly empty: you .... a lot!

d) He's not .... to bed so late. That's why he's tired today.

e) He was given a high honour in .... his services to the country.

f) The trouble is that .... he says, his wife disagrees with him.

g) The instructions said that you .... two pills every four hours.

h) 'I must be going. .... you?'

    'No, I think .... a bit longer.'

4 *For each of the sentences below, write a new sentence as similar as possible in meaning to the original sentence, but using the words given in bold letters. The words must* **not be altered** *in any way.*

    EXAMPLE: His arrival was completely unexpected.
            took

    ANSWER: *His arrival took us completely by surprise.*

a) They don't mind which film they go to.
    matter

    ....

b) He continued his story, even though no one was listening.
    went

    ....

c) If I were left alone, I'd finish the job quickly.
    interrupting

    ....

d) The notice said that you could not smoke in class.
   forbidden

   ....

e) My mother did not like my new shoes.
   disapproved

   ....

f) She was dismissed because her typing was poor.
   lost

   ....

g) He spoke confidently and that impressed me.
   which

   ....

h) She doesn't know the difference between margarine and butter.
   tell

   ....

i) He is famous for his vast knowledge of primitive religion.
   authority

   ....

j) He took no part in the discussion.
   contribute

   ....

SECTION B

5 *Read the following passage, then answer the questions which follow it, basing your answers entirely on the information given in the passage.*

So widespread and accepted is the contemporary passion for sunbathing, and for getting tanned thereby, that it is difficult to remember how recent it is. Up till the nineteen-twenties fashionable ladies would no more have thought of exposing themselves to sunshine than they would today to rain. The sunshade was an essential part of fashionable attire. Now, in all   5
London, you cannot procure one except in theatrical costumiers. Peasants and labourers were liable to be suntanned, but this was just part of their

inelegant way of life. The sign of social distinction was to be pale. How astonished, say, Lily Langtry would have been to know that her successors in high society would go to almost any lengths, including crouching in front 10 of ultra-violet rays and taking tan-producing pills, in order to give an impression of having been baked in the sun!

This cult of the sun, like all others, has been turned to commercial uses. Unguents, oils, special sunbathing attire, bikinis and play-suits and darkened spectacles, have become big business. The largest trade in 15 sunshine, however, is unquestionably done on the French Riviera, now more commonly known as the Côte d'Azur. This narrow coastal strip, never more than twenty kilometres wide, stretching from Menton to Saint Tropez, has become the great temple of the sun-worshippers. Here they come in their millions, thigh-to-thigh on the beaches, bumper-to-bumper on the 20 roads, earnestly engaging in the most ardent of contemporary pursuits – leisure.

It began by being a fashionable winter resort. Russian grand dukes, English actual or would-be aristocrats, American millionaires, the rich from all over Europe, trekked to the Riveria in the winter months to enjoy the 25 clement weather, gamble at the casinos provided for them, and generally demonstrate their superiority to their compatriots who had no alternative but to endure the fogs, frosts and other climatic hazards of their native habitats.

The 1914–18 war and its aftermath put an end to this glorious period, 30 during which the great hotels – Ruhl's, the Negresco, the Hotel de Paris – were built and profitably conducted. The grand dukes disappeared to become taxi-drivers elsewhere; the very rich tended to look for other playgrounds, though there were a few old faithfuls.

The great change, however, was the summer season, which soon 35 attracted many more visitors than the winter one. Hitherto, the Riviera had closed down from April to November. Now hoteliers found the summer more profitable than the winter. The hot sun, which had been their enemy, became a lucrative friend. All along the coast, they edged nearer and nearer to the sea. In the casinos, instead of insisting on 'Smoking', open-necked 40 shirts and even shorts were permissible. Tourist parties made their appearance: lower-class accents were heard and cut-price rather than luxury rates were the order of the day. The better-off type of artisan, now for the first time accorded paid holidays, developed a taste for moving southwards into the sun. Civil servants who had retired on minute 45 pensions were attracted by house property on the Côte d'Azur which was bound to appreciate in value, could always be profitably let, and did not require central heating. Above all, there was camping. Even in 1958, campers totalled 1,800,000. They stayed on an average for twelve days, and brought into the area about a sixth of the total expenditure of 50 holidaymakers there.

a) What is the meaning of 'getting tanned thereby' (line 2)? ....

....

b) What is referred to in the phrase 'you cannot procure one' (line 6)? ....

....

c) Which industries profit from the fashion for sunbathing, according to the
passage? ....

....

....

d) What can you tell from the passage about Lily Langtry? ....

....

e) What is suggested by the phrase 'cult of the sun' (line 13)? ....

....

f) What does the writer mean by a 'trade in sunshine' (lines 15–16)? ....

....

g) Explain the phrases 'thigh-to-thigh on the beaches' (line 20) ....

....

and 'bumper-to-bumper on the roads' (line 20) ....

....

h) What does the word 'it' at the beginning of the third paragraph refer to?

....

....

i) Why were aristocrats from all over Europe attracted to the Riviera? ....

....

....

j) Who are described as having 'no alternative' (line 27)? ....

....

k) Who were the 'few old faithfuls' (line 34)? ....

....

≫→

l) In a paragraph of 70–100 words, summarise the changes mentioned in the last paragraph.

....

....

....

....

....

....

....

....

....

....

....

PAPER 4 LISTENING COMPREHENSION
(31 minutes)

FIRST PART

For questions 1–3 you will hear a conversation between a man in uniform and a passenger at an airport baggage collection point. Tick the box with the correct answer.

1   At the beginning of the conversation the tone of the man's voice suggests he is

A   angry.

B   offhand.

C   callous.

D   upset.

A
B
C
D

2   Why does the passenger say 'Look, I'm sorry . . .'?

A   To make herself heard.

B   To make the man understand.

C   Because she is losing her temper.

D   Because she is about to cry.

A
B
C
D

3   The man changes his attitude because he

A   is frightened of the woman.

B   perceives the woman is mentally unbalanced.

C   is nervous of the manager.

D   realises the woman is becoming distraught.

A
B
C
D

⟫→

SECOND PART

For questions 4–7 you will hear a short passage about the world motor racing championship. Write your answers in the spaces provided.

4   Add the current position of each driver in the world championship in the table below.

Drivers' names	Current position
John Watson	
Keke Rosberg	
Didier Pironi	

5   Why is Pironi unable to win the drivers' championship?

   ....

6   Who will be champion if Watson and Rosberg get the same final total number of points?

   ....

7   Who will be the world champion if Mr Williams' latest appeal succeeds?

   ....

THIRD PART

For questions 8 and 9 you will hear some gardening advice over the telephone.

8   On the notepad below tick the instructions which are correct according to the gardening expert.

Mary, while we're away please remember:

a)   Water plants in greenhouse.

b)   Don't pick runner beans.

c)   Spray leaves of plants.

d)   Water early in the day.

e)   Help yourself to cauliflowers.

f)   Move houseplants to greenhouse.

g)   Put water into growbags.

h)   Look out for fungus diseases.

Thanks a lot – Anne.

9   According to the gardening expert which of these illustrations shows the correct treatment for pot plants while you're away on holiday?

A
B
C
D

FOURTH PART

For questions 10–12 put a tick in one of the boxes A, B, C or D.

10 Since 1971, the number of old people has

    A   about doubled.

    B   remained constant.

    C   increased considerably.

    D   shown a slight increase.

A
B
C
D

11 The author of the document, Anne Good, is dismayed by

    A   the lack of planning.

    B   the old age explosion.

    C   the lack of reliable statistics.

    D   the number of widows.

A
B
C
D

12 According to Anne Good, doctors should

    A   pay more personal attention to elderly patients.

    B   get more assistance from the home helps.

    C   let the hospitals take care of more elderly patients.

    D   leave their elderly patients undisturbed at home.

A
B
C
D

FIFTH PART

For questions 13–17 put a tick in one of the boxes A, B, C or D.

13 Kiri Te Kanawa is very famous. What is she NOT famous as?

    A   A pop singer in New Zealand.

    B   A pop singer in London.

    C   An opera singer in London.

    D   An opera singer in New Zealand.

A
B
C
D

14 David Fingleton thinks that Kiri Te Kanawa

   A   should have made more records before coming to London.

   B   was stupid to come to London.

   C   was right to come to London.

   D   shouldn't have worked in night clubs.

A
B
C
D

15 The other students at the London Opera Centre regarded Kiri as

   A   poorly educated.

   B   too old.

   C   too young.

   D   too affluent.

A
B
C
D

16 Why was life in London hard for Kiri?

   A   She often had to go back to New Zealand.

   B   She wasn't English.

   C   She wasn't used to full-time study.

   D   She preferred pop music.

A
B
C
D

17 David Fingleton says that Kiri Te Kanawa gives her best performances when

   A   she has not prepared a role too thoroughly.

   B   she is in front of an audience.

   C   she is in a recording studio.

   D   she is singing at the Royal Opera House, Covent Garden.

A
B
C
D

PAPER 5   INTERVIEW   (about 15 minutes)

SECTION A: PICTURE CONVERSATION

You will be asked to talk about one of the photographs among the Interview Exercises at the back of this book. Your teacher will tell you which one of the photographs to look at.

SECTION B: READING PASSAGE

You will be asked to read aloud one of the reading passages among the Interview Exercises at the back of this book. Your teacher will tell you which one of the reading passages to look at.

SECTION C: STRUCTURED COMMUNICATION ACTIVITY

You will be asked to take part in a conversation with a group of other students or with your teacher. Your teacher will tell you which section among the Interview Exercises you should look at.

Practice Test 4

PAPER 1 READING COMPREHENSION (1 hour)

This paper is in two parts, section A and section B. For each question you answer correctly in section A you gain **one** *mark; for each question you answer correctly in section B you gain* **two** *marks. No marks are deducted for wrong answers. Answer all the questions. Indicate your choice of answer in each case on the separate sheet which should show your name and examination index number. Follow carefully the instructions about how to record your answer.*

SECTION A

In this section you must choose the word or phrase which best completes each sentence. For each question, 1 to 25, indicate on your answer sheet *the letter A, B, C or D against the number of the question.*

1 The police are .... the town for the missing vehicle.
   A seeking   B looking   C investigating   D combing

2 Though badly damaged by fire, the palace was eventually .... to its original splendour.
   A repaired   B renewed   C restored   D renovated

3 To prevent flooding in winter the water flowing from the dam is constantly .... by a computer.
   A managed   B graded   C monitored   D conducted

4 The government made serious attempts to raise the .... of living.
   A standard   B cost   C level   D mode

5 He is not under arrest, nor have the police placed any .... on his movements.
   A obstacle   B restriction   C veto   D regulation

6 I'm just as .... as you are to make this company successful.
   A dedicated   B serious   C wilful   D determined

7 I've got a very high opinion .... your brother.
   A on   B to   C for   D of

[63]

8 He .... the profits from his speculations to acquire land for his family.
   A gained   B used   C procured   D made

9 He claimed .... from military service because he was a foreign national.
   A liability   B exception   C demobilisation   D exemption

10 The children's bad behaviour in class .... their teacher beyond
    endurance.
    A disturbed   B exasperated   C distracted   D aroused

11 He bought that house, ... that he would inherit money under his
    uncle's will.
    A considering   B assuming   C estimating   D accounting

12 The postal services were .... for several weeks by the strike.
    A disrupted   B perturbed   C disarrayed   D deranged

13 I wished that I could cry but, because of my upbringing I was too ....
    A shy   B inhibited   C rigid   D prevented

14 Since the child had no proper excuse for missing school, her absence should
    be treated as ....
    A desertion   B neglect   C abstention   D truancy

15 All visitors are requested to .... with the regulations.
    A agree   B comply   C assent   D consent

16 This is a most peculiar letter. What do you .... of it?
    A gather   B make   C get   D feel

17 Now that we've identified the problem, we must decide on an appropriate
    course of ....
    A action   B progress   C solution   D development

18 He was blinded by the .... of the approaching car's headlights.
    A glare   B gleam   C glow   D flare

19 Mary gives one account of the conversation, and Fred another; it's difficult
    to .... the two versions.
    A reconcile   B identify   C adjust   D coincide

20 His reputation has been greatly .... by the success of his new book.
    A expanded   B enhanced   C enlarged   D heightened

21 Unless the Prime Minister .... the warning inflation will rise rapidly.
    A remarks   B heeds   D applies   E attends

22 My father hates television and is always .... the disappearance of the
    art of conversation.
    A grieving   B moaning   C complaining   D lamenting

23 When he realised the police had spotted him, the man .... the exit as
    quickly as possible.
    A made off   B made out   C made for   D made up

24 I didn't answer him as it was obvious that he was .... for a fight.
    A intent   B keen   C driving   D spoiling

25 'You may borrow my bicycle .... you are careful with it.'
    A even if   B as long as   C as much as   D expecting

SECTION B

*In this section you will find after each of the passages a number of questions or
unfinished statements about the passage, each with four suggested answers or ways of
finishing. You must choose the one which you think fits best. For each question, 26 to
40, indicate on your answer sheet the letter A, B, C or D against the number of the
question.*

FIRST PASSAGE

The traditional 'widget' is the toy submarine in the cornflake packet. Nowadays
widgets are more likely to be laminated plastic cards, transfers, stick-ons, iron-ons,
or plastic flying saucers. They are, in fact, any of the intriguing articles which are
given away free in packets of something else with the object of persuading children
to persuade their mothers to buy more of the brands in which they are found.

What sort of man works in widgets? Nick Mudie is, on the face of it, much like
any other successful young businessman. Closer acquaintance, however, reveals
that it is not pure chance that has made him the widget expert of the company. He
has a schoolboy's appreciation of the things he works with, a potato crisp
consumer's eye for the widget with the greatest appeal. 'Look' he says, taking from
his desk two identically-sized plastic discs. He tosses the first one, a red plastic
'space star', across the room and shakes his head disapprovingly as it flops at the
end of a silent parabola. 'No earthly good,' he pronounces. 'Now look at this.' And
he takes the green one, fits it on to a rubber band, fits the band on to a plastic ring on
his finger, launches it, and beams delightedly as it spirals upwards, emitting a
high-pitched whizz. 'Now that's a very nice widget indeed.'

The main disadvantage of widgets, in Mudie's eyes, is that instead of selling
his ideas directly to children he has to sell them to logically-minded grown-up
businessmen, who often cannot see that the green whizzing flying saucer is
infinitely superior to the red silent space star. Another problem is that you have to
design widgets which children will like, and which their mothers will also approve

[65]

of. Hence the preponderance of 'educational' widgets which profess to teach a child the history of the Olympics or vertebrate evolution.

The objection to widgets is that if manufacturers are prepared to spend one penny a bag on promoting their crisps, would it not be better just to cut one penny off the price, rather than add some quite unnecessary trinket. In common sense terms, this objection is unanswerable. But widgets – or, come to that, marketing ideas generally – have very little to do with common sense; there is no getting round the fact that a 10p bag of crisps containing a green Martian seems infinitely better value in a child's eyes than a 9p bag containing nothing but crisps.

26 Widgets nowadays are
    A better designed than traditional ones.
    B included in a greater number of products.
    C more varied than they used to be.
    D inferior in value to traditional ones.

27 Nick Mudie's success in his field is attributed to his
    A skill in handling widgets.
    B ability to assess the attraction of a widget.
    C experience in producing widgets.
    D use of children to test the widgets.

28 Mudie regarded the red disc as useless because
    A it didn't work properly.
    B it wasn't interesting enough.
    C it couldn't fly very far.
    D it made an unpleasant noise.

29 Educational widgets are popular because
    A the wide range of subjects appeals to children.
    B they can teach children a subject in depth.
    C they cause less controversy than space toys.
    D they meet the requirements of mothers and children.

30 According to the passage the main factor in successful marketing is
    A selling a product at a realistic price.
    B concentration on quality products.
    C appearing to give value for money.
    D appealing to logically-minded people.

31 'Widgets' could be described as
    A a subtle form of sales technique.
    B an interesting innovation in marketing.
    C a means of distinguishing between the quality of products.
    D a way of controlling the price of products.

SECOND PASSAGE

In spite of his love of theorising, the prehistorian Louis Leakey took nothing for granted and always put everything to a practical test. He became an expert maker of stone tools, and would use them to skin and chop up animals. Even this was not enough: to prove that man had to be a tool-maker to survive, he tried unsuccessfully to skin animals with his teeth.

Louis could show amazing patience if necessary, but by nature he was impetuous. His inclination was to get on with the next job rather than slog over tiresome details. Although temperamentally unsuited to making detailed excavations and minute studies of fossils he did both successfully; he had tremendous self-discipline and would cheerfully work all night if necessary. He was never good at working with other people, especially with men, and always wanted to tackle everything himself.

Although always an individualist and happiest in the bush, he was stimulated by company and blossomed at conferences. He was very adaptable and, curiously, when he lived in Nairobi he enjoyed such suburban pursuits as dog shows and breeding tropical fish. Not gardening, however: this would have been too slow, and for relaxation he preferred to clean a fossil.

Louis had a great ability to make complicated subjects seem straightforward: he loved to share his encyclopaedic knowledge, and however tired he might be, he would respond to an intelligent question. His finds brought him fame in scientific circles, but his way of talking about them made them – and him – known to a much wider public. His frequent appearances on the lecture platform and television screen in the USA, and the articles about him in popular journals brought him an enormous fan-mail. He tried to answer all these letters personally, often arranging to meet the writers if he felt their interest was genuine, and he would go to endless trouble to help anyone he thought worthy of encouragement.

32 Louis Leakey proved that early man was dependent on tools because he himself
   A   mastered the art of making primitive tools.
   B   showed that certain tasks were impossible without tools.
   C   found it unpleasant to skin animals with his teeth.
   D   showed that modern man could survive in primitive conditions.

33 When it came to the more tedious side of his work, Leakey
   A   executed it to the best of his ability.
   B   was too impulsive to work through it properly.
   C   approached it without any motivation.
   D   enjoyed the opportunity for detailed study.

34 During the time that Leakey lived in Nairobi, he
   A   spent a great deal of time at conferences.
   B   carried out research into the fossils of fish.
   C   found it difficult to separate himself from his work.
   D   led a normal kind of existence.

⟫→

35 Leakey's popular success was primarily due to
    A   his exciting discoveries.
    B   his vast knowledge.
    C   his lucid explanations.
    D   his articles in journals.

THIRD PASSAGE

Questions 36 to 40 refer to the following passages.

A   AIRLINE PILOT: Captain Brian Day is one of British Airways' 2,800
   pilots and has worked for the firm for 24 years.
   EARNINGS: In excess of £30,000.
   HOURS: When flying, works 14 days out of 28; when training, works 18
   days out of 28. Long-haul flights mean being away for between three
   and 14 days.
   CONDITIONS: The long and irregular working hours, involving time
   changes, cause physiological problems like difficulty in sleeping.
   PROSPECTS: 'I've reached the top of my profession as a pilot.'

B   TOURIST GUIDE: Gloria Lawrence is a self-employed guide who
   freelances for about ten different companies, taking parties on
   guided tours around London and other places of interest.
   EARNINGS: During her first year about £5,000 gross. Expects more
   in her second year as she becomes more in demand.
   HOURS: Vary from week to week – rough average is about 50
   hours a week.
   CONDITIONS: A lot of tedious coach travel, which can be sticky
   and unpleasant in warm weather. She deals with people all the
   time, talking a great deal and often visiting the same places of
   interest.
   PROSPECTS: 'I would like to do some overseas work, and one day
   organise my own tours.'

C   ESTATE MANAGER: Tony Flick is an estate manager for the small family firm of which he is one of three partners. He runs seven small estates for clients.

EARNINGS: Variable. Last year (a bad year) he earned just over £10,000 gross.

HOURS: 8.30 am–6.30 pm Mondays to Fridays, plus Saturday mornings.

CONDITIONS: Dislikes growing bureaucracy and frequent changes in tax and legislation. 'Coping with all the regulations, such as local planning and the fire and safety regulations, is tremendously time-consuming.'

PROSPECTS: 'I'll stay here till I retire.'

D   TELEPHONE CLEANER: Ivy Bentley is one of 3,000 telephone cleaners employed by a London company. She travels on a regular round, cleaning and disinfecting office telephones.

EARNINGS: Last year her annual earnings reached £2,200 gross, but this included some commission. Operators are paid a percentage on every telephone cleaned.

HOURS: Very flexible, chosen by the operator to suit herself, in agreement with the different firms she visits.

CONDITIONS: Lots of walking and moving around. Visits all sorts of places of work 'from the plush to the fairly grotty'.

PROSPECTS: 'None that I'm looking for.'

36   Which passage, A, B, C or D, describes a person who works regular hours?

37   Which passage, A, B, C or D, describes the best-paid job?

38   In which passage, A, B, C or D, is it admitted that the job can be monotonous?

39   Which passage, A, B, C or D, describes someone who has control over the firm he or she works for?

40   Which passage, A, B, C or D, describes someone who is ambitious about the future?

PAPER 2   COMPOSITION   (2 hours)

Write two only of the following composition exercises. Your answers must follow exactly the instructions given. Write in pen, not pencil. You are allowed to make alterations, but see that your work is clear and easy to read.

1   Describe some of your earliest memories. (About 350 words)

2   Is it right to eat meat? Give your reasons. (About 350 words)

3   A television programme that seemed to you definitely harmful. (About 200 words)

4   You are personnel manager of a company and you receive the following letter from one of your directors:

> Dear John,
>
> We need a new Sales Manager to deal with the sales side of our chain stores. The sort of chap I have in mind should be able to get people cracking on the job without putting their backs up. He should have had a lot of similar experience, but shouldn't have one foot in the grave. He won't be able to sit in his office all day long, because, as you know, we're spread over three continents. We'll pay him well, and extra if his results are good. The usual extras go with the job, such as a car on the company, pension (he doesn't pay), life insurance, expenses etc. This is a fairly high-powered job, and the sky's the limit.
>
> Many thanks,
>
> Yours

Write an advertisement of about 100 words for insertion in a newspaper, concerning the vacancy. Include in suitable form all the details mentioned in the above letter. Be brief, but do not use abbreviations.

5   Basing your answer on your reading of the prescribed text concerned, answer
    one of the following. (About 350 words)

    SHAKESPEARE: *Richard II*
    'You may my glories and my state depose,
    But not my griefs; still am I King of those.'
    What elements in Shakespeare's portrait of Richard do you notice in this
    quotation?

    J. M. SYNGE: *The Playboy of the Western World and Riders to the Sea*
    What pleasures, as well as difficulties, have you found in studying these
    plays, which are not in a standard form of English?

    MARGARET DRABBLE: *The Waterfall*
    'Dialogues in a sick room, in claustrophobic proximity. Dependence,
    confinement, solicitude.' How accurately does this describe the book?

PAPER 3   USE OF ENGLISH   (2 hours)

SECTION A

1   *Fill each of the numbered blanks in the following passage with* **one** *suitable word.*

Altruism is the performance of an unselfish act. As a pattern of behaviour this act .... (1) have two properties: it must benefit someone .... (2) and it must do so .... (3) the disadvantage of the benefactor. It is .... (4) merely a matter of being helpful, it is helpfulness .... (5) a cost to yourself. Since human beings are animals .... (6) ancestors have won the long struggle .... (7) survival during their evolutionary history, ... (8) cannot be genetically programmed .... (9) display true altruism. Evolution theory suggests that they must, like all .... (10) animals, be entirely selfish .... (11) their actions, even .... (12) they appear to be at their most self-sacrificing and philanthropic. This is the biological, evolutionary argument and it is completely convincing .... (13) far as it .... (14) but it does not seem to explain many .... (15) mankind's 'finer moments'. If a man sees a burning house and .... (16) it his small daughter, an old friend, a complete stranger, or .... (17) a screaming kitten, he may, ... (18) pausing to think, ... (19) headlong into the building and be badly .... (20) in a desperate attempt to save a life.

2   *Finish each of the following sentences in such a way that it means exactly the same as the sentence printed before it.*

   EXAMPLE: Immediately after his arrival, things went wrong.

   ANSWER: No sooner *had he arrived than things went wrong.*

a) Their dog was so fierce that nobody would visit them.

They had ....

b) That dress has only the slightest mark on it.

I can barely ....

c) He insisted on a full apology.

Nothing but ....

d) He remembered, and so did she.

He didn't ....

e) My decision to get up and dance coincided with the band's decision to stop playing.

The moment ....

f) The doctor advised me to rest.

The doctor suggested ....

g) They had to wait for twelve hours before their flight left.

Only after a ....

h) Their teacher is making them study hard.

They are ....

i) They were just as good as we had expected.

They certainly lived ....

j) Even though I admire his courage, I think he is foolish.

Much ....

3 *Fill each of the blanks with a suitable word or phrase.*

EXAMPLE: Even if I had stood on a chair, *I wouldn't have been able to reach the light bulb.*

a) You didn't have to go by bus. You .... my car.

b) He drove past at a terrific speed. He must .... at least 90 m.p.h.

[73]

⟫→

c) He doesn't like repairing the car himself. He prefers .... by a mechanic.

d) What are you doing here? Aren't you .... at work today?

e) Had I known you were coming, I .... something for you to eat.

f) Clever ...., he still wasn't able to find a solution to the problem.

g) I wish you .... with us to Greece. It won't be any fun without you.

h) There you are! I .... you everywhere.

4 *For each of the sentences below, write a new sentence as similar as possible in meaning to the original sentence, but using the words given in bold letters. The words must **not be altered** in any way.*

  EXAMPLE: His arrival was completely unexpected.
           took

  ANSWER: *His arrival took us completely by surprise.*

a) How do you explain the difference between the two witnesses' stories?
   account

   ....

b) He is certainly not stupid.
   means

   ....

c) 'You don't appreciate me,' she complained.
   granted

   ....

d) After the death of the giant they lived in peace.
   once

   ....

e) The man in that painting bears a strong resemblance to my uncle.
   reminds

   ....

f) Someone has stolen her bicycle.
   had

   ....

g) People knew they were spies.
known

....

h) I found it when I was looking through some old papers.
came

....

i) We didn't go in case we were recognised.
fear

....

j) After two hours the bridegroom still hadn't appeared.
sign

....

SECTION B

5 *Read the following passage, then answer the questions which follow it, basing your answers entirely on the information given in the passage.*

The thing that would astonish anyone coming for the first time into the service quarters of a hotel would be the fearful noise and disorder during the rush hours. It is something so different from the steady work in a shop or factory that it looks at first sight like mere bad management. But it is really quite unavoidable, and for this reason; hotel work is not particularly 5
hard, but by its nature it comes in rushes and cannot be economised. You cannot, for instance, grill a steak two hours before it is wanted; you have to wait till the last moment, by which time a mass of other work has accumulated, and then do it all together, in frantic haste. The result is that at mealtimes everyone is doing two men's work, which is impossible without 10
noise and quarrelling. Indeed, the quarrels are a necessary part of the process, for the pace would never be kept up if everyone did not accuse everyone else of idling. It was for this reason that during rush hours at the Hotel Splendide the whole staff raged and cursed like demons. But they were not losing their heads and wasting time; they were just stimulating 15
one another for the effort of packing four hours' work into two hours.

What keeps a hotel going is the fact that the employees take a genuine pride in their work, beastly and silly though it is. If a man idles, the others soon find him out, and conspire against him to get him sacked. Cooks, waiters and 'plongeurs' – the vegetable peelers and pot scourers – differ in 20
outlook, but they are all proud of their efficiency.

Undoubtedly the most workmanlike class, and the least servile, are the cooks. They do not earn quite so much as waiters, but their prestige is higher and their employment steadier. The cook does not look upon himself as a servant, but as a skilled workman. He knows his power – knows that he alone makes or mars a restaurant, and that if he is five minutes late everything is out of gear. He despises the whole non-cooking staff, and makes it a point of honour to insult everyone below the head waiter. It is not the cooking that is so difficult, but the doing everything to time. Between breakfast and luncheon the head cook at the Hotel Splendide would receive orders for several hundred dishes, all to be served at different times; he cooked few of them himself, but he gave instructions about all of them and inspected them before they were sent up. It is for their punctuality, and not for any superiority in technique, that men cooks are preferred to women.

The waiter's outlook is quite different. He too is proud of his skill, but his skill is chiefly in being servile. His work gives him the mentality, not of a workman, but of a snob. He lives perpetually in the sight of rich people, stands at their tables, listens to their conversations, sucks up to them with smiles and discreet little jokes. He has the pleasure of spending money by proxy. Between constantly seeing money, and hoping to get it, the waiter comes to identify himself to some extent with the customer. He will take pains to serve a meal in style, because he feels that he is participating in the meal himself. He finds the servile nature of his work rather congenial.

The plongeurs, who perform most of the hard manual tasks in the kitchen, see things differently. Their job offers no prospects, is intensely exhausting and has not a trace of skill or interest. They have to be constantly on the run, and to put up with long hours and a stuffy atmosphere. They have no way of escaping from this life, for they cannot save a penny from their wages. And yet the plongeurs have a kind of pride. It is the pride of the drudge – the man who is equal to no matter what quantity of hard work.

a) What are the 'service quarters' (line 2) of a hotel? ....

....

....

b) Explain the phrase 'steady work' (line 3). ....

....

c) What does 'it' refer to in line 4? ....

....

d) What does the example of the steak reveal about hotel work?..............................

....

....

e) What does 'which' refer to in line 10? ....

....

f) What was the effect of the quarrels on the people preparing food at the Hotel Splendide?

....

....

....

....

g) What is the importance of the fact that the hotel staff take pride in their work?

....

....

....

....

h) Explain the phrase 'makes or mars' (line 26). ....

....

....

i) How does the head cook behave towards the rest of the hotel staff? ....

....

....

j) Apart from actually cooking, what were the daily duties of the head cook at the Hotel Splendide?

....

....

....

....

k) What does the passage imply about women as cooks? ....

....

....

....

l) What is meant by the phrase 'by proxy' (lines 40–41)? ....

....

....

....

....

m) What is the effect of the 'plongeurs' being so badly paid? ....

....

....

....

n) In a paragraph of 50–100 words, summarise the attitudes of the three classes of hotel employees to their jobs.

....

....

....

....

....

....

....

....

....

....

....

....

PAPER 4   LISTENING COMPREHENSION
(31 minutes)

FIRST PART

For questions 1–6 you will hear a radio interview about tattooing. Tick the box with the correct answer.

1   Today in Britain, tattooing is

    A   becoming more fashionable.

    B   regarded as sentimental.

    C   regarded as an art form.

    D   the subject of exhibitions in London.

A
B
C
D

2   What tattoos does Dick have?

    A   Animals and birds.

    B   Animals and words.

    C   Birds and words.

    D   Birds and machines.

A
B
C
D

3   Where are his tattoos?

    A   On his left arm.

    B   On his right and left arms.

    C   On his arms and chest.

    D   On his arms, chest and back.

A
B
C
D

4   According to Dick, if a cat scratches you

    A   you bleed a great deal.

    B   it hurts less than being tattooed.

    C   it punctures less than four layers of skin.

    D   the slight sharpness disappears quickly.

A
B
C
D

»»→

5 If you cry while you are being tattooed

   A the tattooist will be impressed.

   B he will think you have a thick skin.

   C you will not have to pay.

   D the tattooist will try to forget the experience.

A
B
C
D

6 What point does Ron Aldridge make about tattooing?

   A It is a primitive technique.

   B It is very beautiful.

   C It is something we have always done.

   D It is impossible to remove.

A
B
C
D

SECOND PART

For questions 7–9 you will hear a radio interview with a doctor. Tick the correct answer in the boxes provided.

7 According to the doctor phobias cause people to experience

   A great excitement.

   B severe headaches.

   C physical sensations.

   D complete exhaustion.

A
B
C
D

8 The doctor talks about working in cold storage in order to

   A explain what she means by 'condition'.

   B show that we cannot control our emotions.

   C prove that phobias are not uncommon.

   D explain what she means by 'sensitive'.

A
B
C
D

9 Most phobias are rooted in

   A fears of travelling.

   B childhood experiences.

   C rational fears.

   D social problems.

A
B
C
D

THIRD PART

For questions 10 – 13 you will hear part of a programme about the manufacture of glass bottles. Tick the correct answers in the boxes provided.

10   Which costs are said to be increasing in the bottle manufacturing industry?
     Tick **one or more** boxes.

   basic ingredients

   labour

   fuel

   advertising

11   How do today's bottles differ from those of the past?
     Tick **one or more** boxes.

   more attractive

   more exact size

   heavier

   thicker

12 According to Mr Pearson, how are the mixed ingredients transferred to the furnace? Tick **one** of the boxes A, B, C or D.

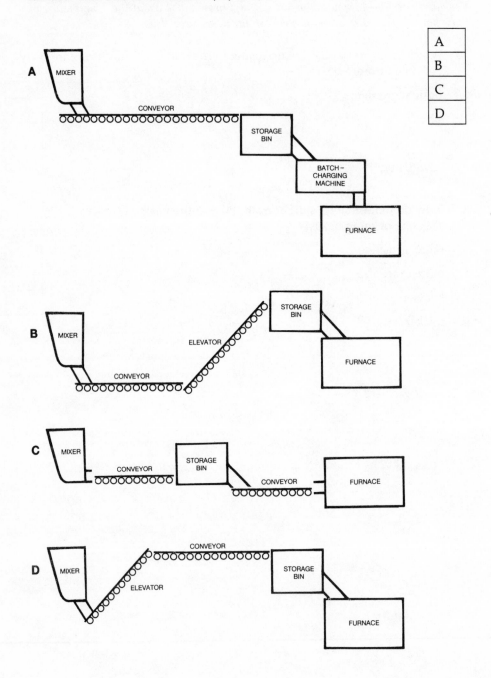

13 Why is the glass heated to a temperature of 1,550 degrees Centigrade? Tick **one** box.

A To clear the furnace.	A
B To prevent the batch components melting.	B
C To produce bubbles of air.	C
D To purify the glass.	D

FOURTH PART

For questions 14 and 15 you will hear a weather report.

14 Temperature – **tick one box for each period** (the day of the 19th has been done for you).

	This afternoon	Tonight	Tomorrow	Tomorrow night
over 5°C				
0°C–5°C			✓	
below 0°C (frost)				
below −5°C (heavy frost)				

15 Coastal conditions at night – **tick two of the boxes.**

colder than inland	
warmer than inland	
windier than inland	
less windy than inland	

PAPER 5 INTERVIEW (about 15 minutes)

SECTION A: PICTURE CONVERSATION

You will be asked to talk about one of the photographs among the Interview
Exercises at the back of this book. Your teacher will tell you which one of the
photographs to look at.

SECTION B: READING PASSAGE

You will be asked to read aloud one of the reading passages among the
Interview Exercises at the back of this book. Your teacher will tell you which one
of the reading passages to look at.

SECTION C: STRUCTURED COMMUNICATION ACTIVITY

You will be asked to take part in a conversation with a group of other students
or with your teacher. Your teacher will tell you which section among the
Interview Exercises you should look at.

Practice Test 5

PAPER 1   READING COMPREHENSION   (1 hour)

*This paper is in two parts, section A and section B. For each question you answer correctly in section A you gain **one** mark; for each question you answer correctly in section B you gain **two** marks. No marks are deducted for wrong answers. Answer all the questions. Indicate your choice of answer in each case on the separate sheet which should show your name and examination index number. Follow carefully the instructions about how to record your answer.*

SECTION A

In this section you must choose the word or phrase which best completes each sentence. For each question, 1 to 25, indicate on your answer sheet the letter A, B, C or D against the number of the question.

1 Armed terrorists are reported to have .... the Embassy.
   A taken up   B taken to   C taken over   D taken into

2 I should be most grateful if you would give me a .... of this new typewriter.
   A demonstration   B display   C showing   D manifestation

3 How many people do you think his car would ....?
   A occupy   B hold   C fit   D load

4 His mother's illness had placed him under a considerable ....
   A tension   B strain   C stress   D worry

5 The other transport unions gave the railway workers their ....
   A agreement   B solidarity   C backing   D alliance

6 Conditions today didn't suit this jockey, but the course tomorrow should be much more to his ....
   A liking   B approval   C talent   D benefit

7 As a result of his father's death, he .... a lot of money.
   A came into   B came over   C came to   D came through

8　He has been given work as a window cleaner even though he has no
　　..................... for heights.
　　A head　　B skill　　C ability　　D balance

9　As we belong to different political parties, there is a great .... between
　　my views and yours.
　　A chink　　B gorge　　C gulf　　D space

10　Teachers have learned to take shortages of text books and equipment in
　　their ....
　　A stride　　B scope　　C habit　　D course

11　She always prided herself on being a .... judge of character.
　　A shrewd　　B cunning　　C grave　　D solid

12　The boy's parents were prepared to go to any .... to keep his name out
　　of the papers.
　　A ways　　B depths　　C measures　　D lengths

13　The prison was so well guarded that any thought of escape was ....
　　A despairing　　B aimless　　C desperate　　D pointless

14　Financial worries gradually .... his health and he was obliged to retire
　　early.
　　A undermined　　B disabled　　C exhausted　　D invalidated

15　He was disappointed by his result, but he is now .... to having to
　　re-take the exam.
　　A composed　　B submitted　　C reconciled　　D subdued

16　Although he claims to have left his job voluntarily, he was actually ....
　　for misconduct.
　　A resigned　　B released　　C dispelled　　D dismissed

17　It suddenly .... his mind that he had forgotten to tell his wife he would
　　be late.
　　A passed　　B filled　　C crossed　　D occurred

18　..................... I know the money is safe I shall not worry about it.
　　A Even though　　B Unless　　C As long as　　D However

19　He joined the party as an idealistic young man, but was totally .... by
　　the cynicism he found there.
　　A disillusioned　　B contemptuous　　C disinterested　　D disbelieving

20 People become less .... to new ideas as they grow older.
   A receptive   B available   C hospitable   D attractive

21 Having considered the problem for a while she thought better .... her first solution.
   A to   B than   C from   D of

22 'How could you let the baby climb the stairs? I am surprised .... you!'
   A with   B at   C for   D on

23 Is he really .... to judge a brass band contest?
   A competent   B skilful   C capable   D efficient

24 If you weren't satisfied, you .... have complained to the manager.
   A can   B could   C need   D will

25 Most people can't .... the day without at least one cup of tea or coffee.
   A get through   B get on   C get at   D get by

SECTION B

In this section you will find after each of the passages a number of questions or unfinished statements about the passage, each with four suggested answers or ways of finishing. You must choose the one which you think fits best. For each question, 26 to 40, indicate on your answer sheet the letter A, B, C or D against the number of the question.

FIRST PASSAGE

I have had just about enough of being treated like a second-class citizen, simply because I happen to be that put-upon member of society – a customer. The more I go into shops and hotels, banks and post offices, railway stations, airports and the like, the more I'm convinced that things are being run solely to suit the firm, the system, or the union. There seems to be an insidious new motto for so-called 'service' organisations – Staff Before Service.

How often, for example, have you queued for what seems like hours at the Post Office or the supermarket because there weren't enough staff on duty to man all the service grilles or checkout counters? Surely in these days of high unemployment it must be possible to recruit cashiers and counter staff? Yet supermarkets, hinting darkly at higher prices, claim that unshrouding all their cash registers at any one time would increase overheads. And the Post Office says we cannot expect all their service grilles to be occupied 'at times when demand is low'.

It's the same with hotels. Because waiters and kitchen staff must finish when it suits *them*, dining rooms close earlier or menu choice is curtailed. As for us guests (and how the meaning of that word has been whittled away), we just have to put up with it. There's also the nonsense of so many friendly hotel night porters having been phased out in the interests of 'efficiency' (i.e. profits) and replaced by coin-guzzling machines which dispense everything from lager to laxatives. Not to mention the creeping menace of the tea-making kit in your room: a kettle with an assortment of teabags, plastic milk cartons and lump sugar. Who wants to wake up to a raw teabag? I don't, especially when I am paying for 'service'.

Can it be halted, this erosion of service, this growing attitude that the customer is always a nuisance? I fervently hope so because it's happening, sadly, in all walks of life.

Our only hope is to hammer home our indignation whenever and wherever we can and, if all else fails, resurrect that other, older slogan – and Take Our Custom Elsewhere.

26 The writer feels that nowadays a customer is
    A the recipient of privileged treatment.
    B unworthy of proper consideration.
    C classified by society as inferior.
    D the victim of modern organisations.

27 In the writer's opinion, the quality of service is changing because
    A the customers' demands have changed.
    B the staff receive more consideration than the customers.
    C the customers' needs have increased.
    D the staff are less considerate than their employers.

28 According to the writer, long queues at counters are caused by
    A difficulties in recruiting staff.
    B inadequate staffing arrangements.
    C staff being made redundant.
    D lack of co-operation staff.

29 Service organisations claim that keeping the checkout counters manned would result in
    A a rise in the price for providing services.
    B demands by cashiers for more money.
    C insignificant benefits for the customers.
    D the need to purchase expensive equipment.

30 The disappearance of old-style hotel porters can be attributed to the fact that
    A few people are willing to do this type of work.
    B machines are more reliable than human beings.
    C the personal touch is appreciated less nowadays.
    D automation has provided cheaper alternatives.

SECOND PASSAGE

There have been three periods in the history of post-war broadcast interviewing. The first, 'the age of deference', when it was an honour to have you, the interviewee, on the programme, lasted until the middle 50s. The second, 'the age of ascendancy', when politicians in particular looked upon the interviewers as agenda-setting rivals who made them feel uncomfortable by their knowledge and rigour of questioning, came to an end at the beginning of this decade. Now we are in 'the age of evasion', when most prominent interviewees have acquired the art of seeming to answer a question whilst bypassing its essential thrust.

Why should this be? From the complexity of causes responsible for the present mediocrity of the interview form, a few are worth singling out, such as the revolt against rationality and the enthronement of feeling in its place. To the young of the 60s, the painstaking search for understanding of a given political problem may have appeared less fruitful and satisfying than the unfettered ventilation of emotion which the same problem generated. Sooner or later, broadcasting was bound to reflect this.

This bias against understanding has continued. To this we must add the professional causes that have played their part. The convention of the broadcast interview has undergone little change or radical development since its rise in the 50s. When a broadcasting form ceases to develop, its practitioners tend to take it for granted and are likely to say 'how' rather than ask 'why'.

Furthermore, these partly psychological, partly professional tendencies were greatly accelerated by the huge expansion of news and current affairs output over the last 15 years. When you had many additional hours of current affairs broadcasting, interviewing turned out to be a far cheaper convention than straight reporting, which is costly in terms of permanent reporters and time preparation. The temptation to combine an expanded news and current affairs service with a relatively small additional financial outlay by making the interview ubiquitous proved overwhelming.

To be fair, there are compensating virtues in interviewing, such as immediacy and authority, yet in all honesty I must say that the spread of the interviewing format has led to a corresponding diminution of quality broadcasting.

31 According to the author, in the past politicians thought that television interviewers
   A knew more about politics than they did.
   B should be honoured to meet them.
   C really aspired to be politicians too.
   D gave them a difficult time in interviews.

32 In the 60s young people
   A talked about problems instead of solving them.
   B found political problems too difficult to understand.
   C preferred the expression of feeling to logical argument.
   D were dissatisfied with the standard of interviewing.

≫→

33 From a professional standpoint, one reason for the decline in the quality of the interview is that
   A people are not so interested in politics.
   B interviewing techniques have remained much the same.
   C people are not so radical as in the 60s.
   D broadcasters consider the interview format outmoded.

34 Compared with other forms of current affairs programmes, interviews are
   A shorter and more efficient.
   B more carefully prepared.
   C fairer in their approach.
   D more authentic and direct.

35 The writer believes that because of the increasing use of interviews
   A there are too many current affairs programmes.
   B standards in broadcasting have declined.
   C the cost of broadcasting has increased.
   D broadcasters have become less popular.

THIRD PASSAGE

Questions 36 to 40 refer to the following passages.

A Cheats at cooking never own deep-freezers; it's far too much sweat first getting things frozen and then unfreezing them again. The freezing compartment of your fridge, however, should always be as well-stocked as you can keep it. Ice-cream, for instance, should always be available so that you need never be short of a dessert.

B Freezing is the simplest and most convenient way of keeping food at home, and the only method of preservation which doesn't change the way the food looks or tastes. When the freezer is stocked, you will have permanently on hand in the kitchen a wide selection of 'fresh food'.
   Owning a freezer has been compared to having a supermarket at home and this is no exaggeration. By reaching into the cabinet at any time you should be able to select exactly those food items or meals you need.

C Also I'm not convinced freezing does always save money. Each time I am reminded that 20 per cent of the population are freezer owners I console myself with the thought that there are still 80 per cent who are not. My main grumble is that unless you understand temperature control with almost scientific dedication freezing causes loss of flavour, and as a cook I spend a great deal of time and effort nurturing flavour. Having said this, it is true you can save a little money with fruit and vegetables, if you grow these yourself and produce too much for your immediate needs. If you already have a freezer and it's saving you money, it can't be a bad thing.

D Novice freezer owners tend to think only in terms of preserving raw materials such as home-grown fruit and vegetables, or fresh poultry and game. Experience brings the knowledge that frozen prepared dishes are invaluable to the busy housewife or career woman, to those who entertain a lot, and even to those who live alone. It is an economy in both shopping and cooking time to prepare dishes in bulk for future use.

36 In which passage, A, B, C or D, does the writer consider that freezing spoils food?

37 Which passage, A, B, C or D, suggests that freezer owners should cook large quantities of food at a time?

38 In which passage, A, B, C or D, is it considered that freezers create too much work?

39 In which passage, A, B, C or D, is it stated that freezers can save time?

40 Which passage, A, B, C or D, stresses the advantage of keeping a freezer full?

PAPER 2 COMPOSITION (2 hours)

*Write **two only** of the following composition exercises. Your answers must follow exactly the instructions given. Write in pen, not pencil. You are allowed to make alterations, but see that your work is clear and easy to read.*

1 Describe a visit to *either* a disco *or* a street market. (About 350 words)

2 What are the qualities of a perfect husband? (About 350 words)

3 The foreign country you would most like to live in, and why. (About 200 words)

4 A textbook gives the following 'design pointers' for electric food mixers. Write, in about 200 words, a detailed account of your experiences in trying out a particular model which failed to meet the requirements mentioned:

> Adequate size for purpose
> Can deal with large and small amounts of mixtures satisfactorily
> Beaters easy to insert and remove
> Enough attachments to meet needs
> Attachments easy to fix and use
> Controls clearly marked and definite in action, easy to use
> All parts easy to clean
> Sound, safe construction, motor has adequate power
> Sufficient flex for needs

5 Basing your answer on your reading of the prescribed text concerned, answer *one* of the following. (About 350 words)

DICKENS: *David Copperfield*
It has been said that Dickens told more of the emotional truths of growing up than anyone else before Freud. What do you think of his portrayal of childhood?

J. M. SYNGE: *The Playboy of the Western World and Riders to the Sea*
Synge said that both the bad and the good in the Irish peasant came from 'the richness of their nature – a thing that is precious beyond words'. How do his plays bring out this quality?

MARGARET DRABBLE: *The Waterfall*
'It won't, of course, do: as an account, I mean, of what took place.' Discuss the way Jane's story is told.

PAPER 3   USE OF ENGLISH   (2 hours)

SECTION A

1   *Fill each of the numbered blanks in the following passage with* **one** *suitable word.*

New technologies, like all technologies, are morally neutral. .... (1)

their advent .... (2) the world a better place or .... (3)

depends on the uses to which they are .... (4). And that,

.... (5) turn, depends upon .... (6) decisions of many

people, especially of politicians, managers, trade .... (7) leaders,

engineers .... (8) scientists. The new technologies, cheap, flexible,

dependent .... (9) knowledge and information as their main input,

can .... (10) human being from many .... (11) their

current constraints, ... (12) example constraints of resources and

geography. .... (13)   the   new   technologies   could   also

.... (14) those with power to control their fellow citizens even

.... (15) effectively than in the .... (16) efficient

dictatorships .... (17) the past. The new technological society

will .... (18) colossal demands on our imagination and ingenuity

and   on   the   capacity   .... (19)   our   institutions   to   respond

.... (20) new challenges.

2   *Finish each of the following sentences in such a way that it means exactly the same as the sentence printed before it.*

   EXAMPLE: I expect that he will get there by lunchtime.

   ANSWER: I expect him   *to get there by lunchtime.*

   a)   Would you mind not smoking in here?

        I'd rather ....

b) No matter how hard I tried I couldn't open the door.

Try ....

c) The critics were very impressed by her performance.

Her performance made ....

d) When are the council going to do something about the city's traffic problems?

It's high time something ....

e) I didn't realise who he was until later.

Only later ....

f) The value of sterling has fallen considerably in the past week.

There has ....

g) It won't make any difference if it rains because we'll still go.

We'll still go ....

h) We left quietly, so that we wouldn't disturb the children.

So as ....

i) I would do anything for you.

There's ....

j) Given fair warning, I could have avoided that date.

If you had told me ....

3   *Fill each of the blanks with a suitable word or phrase*

     EXAMPLE: Even if I had stood on a chair, *I wouldn't have been able to reach the light bulb.*

a) Our dog was so ill that we .... put down by the vet.

b) Once he's been there a few weeks, Richard .... used to his new school.

c) My uncle's been dead for years. You .... seen him yesterday.

d) 'I'm very strong.'

'I don't believe you. .... see you lift that suitcase.'

e) I shall resign .... to accept my proposal.

f) The plane was due at 9.45. It .... landed by now.

g) Listening to the radio is a good way of .... yourself informed about current affairs.

h) In spite .... the bus he still arrived on time.

i) If you had been in that situation, ... taken?

4 *For each of the sentences below, write a new sentence as similar as possible in meaning to the original sentence, but using the words given in bold letters. The words must **not be altered** in any way.*

EXAMPLE: John inflated the tyres of his bicycle.
blew

ANSWER: *John blew up the tyres of his bicycle.*

a) We could just discern the buildings through the fog.
make

....

b) It is my strong belief that John was responsible.
suspect

....

c) He has a good relationship with all his students.
gets

....

d) His rude behaviour is too much for me.
put

....

e) The meeting was well attended.
turned

....

f) It was obvious that the old house was past its prime.
days

....

⟫→

g) As a boy, he was a regular churchgoer.
used

....

h) How likely is it she will pass the exam?
chances

....

i) The film didn't come up to my expectations.
short

....

j) I can't stand that dreadful noise any longer.
enough

....

SECTION B

5 *Read the following passage, then answer the questions which follow it, basing your answers entirely on the information given in the passage.*

Everyone nowadays knows that air photographs have contributed enormously to the discovery and elucidation of archaeological sites, yet there is nothing mysterious or complicated about the basic principle of archaeology from the air. The late Dr O. G. S. Crawford made a convenient and striking demonstration when he published side by side two photographs of a   5
patterned carpet, seen (as he put it) first from the cat's-eye and then from the man's-eye viewpoint. The cat, a few inches above the carpet, sees a small area at a very oblique angle, which gives no indication of the structure of the total pattern, easily perceived by the man looking down on the carpet from a height. This is exactly what happens in air observation, but the value   10
of air photographs is twofold. While they enable comprehensive views to be obtained which are impossible on the ground, and thus enable the significance of features to be recognised, they also reveal sites and features which are completely invisible on the ground.

Features invisible on the ground may be shown in air photographs in   15
three ways: by shadows, by crop marks, and by soil marks. Almost completely flattened features, such as ploughed-out banks or mounds, may be shown up by air photographs taken with a very low sun; such shadows in most cases are not observed or appreciated when seen from the ground, but become obvious in the comprehensive view given by an air   20
photograph. Crop marks depend on differential growth over underlying features. Over buried walls the crop will tend to be poorer and more

stunted, while over the deep soil of a filled-in ditch it will be more luxuriant. Such differences may be so marked as to show up from the mere height of the crop, or even as shadow marks. But the differences are much more 25 marked at the time when the crop is starting to ripen, or the grass to become parched. The crop or grass with shallow roots, owing to underlying walls, will turn yellow sooner, and *vice versa*, and if the photograph is taken at just the right moment, will show up clearly.

'Soil marks' is the term used to describe actual differences in the colour 30 of the soil as revealed when a field is freshly ploughed. For instance, when the material in a bank has been obtained from a ditch which penetrates underlying chalk, traces of the bank can be detected as a band of chalky soil, usually much broader than the original bank because of the spreading effect of the plough. 35

The uses of air photographs in surveys and as an adjunct to excavation are readily apparent, and they have added enormously to archaeological knowledge.

a) What does the writer mean by 'archaeology from the air' (lines 3–4)?

....

....

b) What did the photographs of the carpet demonstrate? ....

....

c) What does 'this' (line 10) refer to? ....

....

d) What does 'comprehensive' (line 11) mean in this context?

....

e) Why are some banks and mounds 'almost completely flattened' (lines 16–17)?

....

....

....

f) What is meant by 'a very low sun' (line 18) and why should it help to reveal certain features?

....

....

....

⟫⟶

g) What is 'differential growth' (line 21) and what are its causes? ....

....

....

....

....

h) Give two examples from the passage of 'underlying features' (lines 21–22).

....

....

i) What word could replace 'marked' in lines 24 and 26? ....

j) According to the sentence 'Such differences . . . shadow marks' (lines 24–25), what technique may not be necessary in order to see the differences mentioned?

....

....

k) Replace the phrase *vice versa* (line 28) with an appropriate sentence of your own.

....

....

l) When exactly is 'just the right moment' (lines 28–29)? ....

....

m) What is it that will 'show up clearly' (line 29)? ....

....

n) Briefly explain the formation of soil marks (line 30). ....

....

....

....

o) In a paragraph of 80–100 words summarise the ways in which air photographs can help the archaeologist.

....

....

....

....

....

....

....

....

PAPER 4   LISTENING COMPREHENSION
(32 minutes)

FIRST PART

For each of the following statements about the earthquake tick one box to show whether it is true or false.

	True	False
1 It caused an electricity failure in the capital.		
2 It caused damage to buildings.		
3 It was more powerful than the one in the previous year.		
4 It caused thousands of injuries.		
5 65 people were killed in last year's earthquake.		
6 The earthquake devastated the resort of Cancun.		
7 An international conference was taking place when it occurred.		
8 It caused a bridge to collapse.		
9 The British and Chinese leaders were in Mexico when it occurred.		
10 It caused the British and Chinese leaders to cancel their talks with the Mexican President.		

[100]

SECOND PART

For the next part of the test you will hear a gardening expert.

11 Tick **one or more** boxes to show which cuttings are prepared correctly.

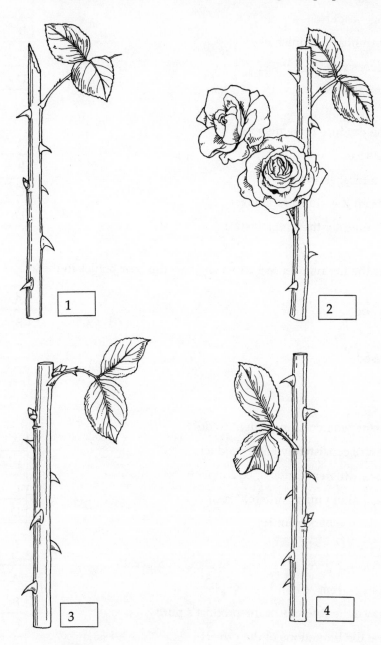

THIRD PART

For each of questions 12–17 put a tick in one of the boxes A, B, C or D.

12 Who is being interviewed?

A   a village leader

B   a government administrator

C   a businessman

D   a visiting expert

A
B
C
D

13 How is the produce to be disposed of?

A   sold abroad

B   sold in local shops

C   sold from the villagers' houses

D   distributed by the kitchen staff

A
B
C
D

14 How does the interviewer feel when she sees the beer bottles in the factory?

A   surprised

B   annoyed

C   confused

D   shocked

A
B
C
D

15 What are the women being taught to do?

A   to ensure consistently good products

B   to make different kinds of equipment

C   to learn about many different recipes

D   to make use of old bottles

A
B
C
D

16 The interviewee gives his rules of hygiene in order to

A   explain current scientific principles.

B   convince the listeners of the product's purity.

C   excuse the limitations of the project.

D   describe the purity of the water supply.

A
B
C
D

17   The eventual aim of the project is to

    A   make the villagers self-sufficient.

    B   produce guidelines for future developments.

    C   make sure there are sufficient raw materials.

    D   teach the villagers the principles of hygiene.

A
B
C
D

FOURTH PART

For each of the questions 18–22 put a tick in one of the boxes A, B, C or D.

18   What does LISA stand for?

    A   LOWER INTEGRATED SOFTWARE ARCHIVE

    B   LOCAL INTEGRATED SOFTWARE ARCHIVE

    C   LOCAL INTEGRATED SOFTWARE ARCHITECTURE

    D   LOWER INTEGRATED SOFTWARE ARCHITECTURE

A
B
C
D

19   Which of these diagrams best represents the LISA computer system?

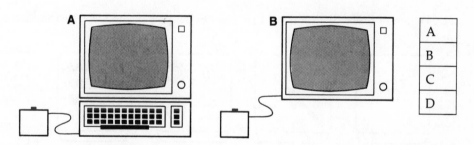

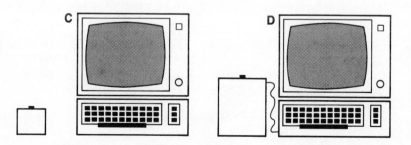

A
B
C
D

20 Which of these diagrams best represents the special feature of the LISA screen?

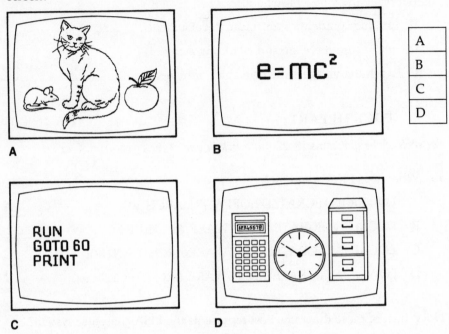

A   B   C   D

A   B   C   D

21 Which of these diagrams best represents the part of the LISA system that you move with your hand?

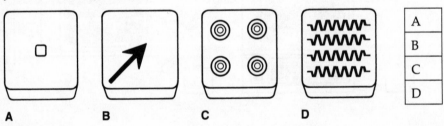

A   B   C   D

A   B   C   D

22 Which of the following pictures best represents the way a person would use the LISA Mouse?

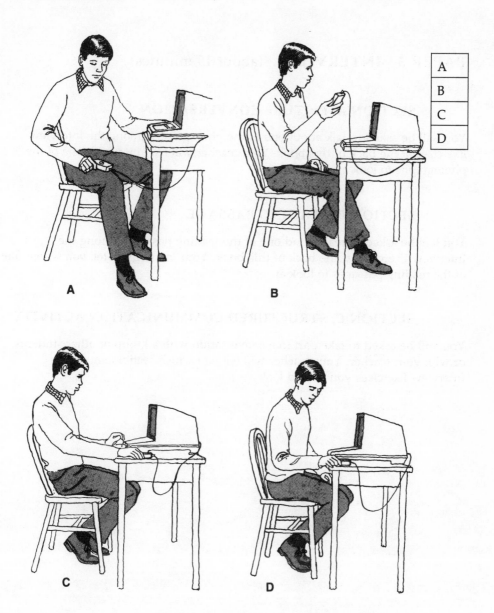

PAPER 5 INTERVIEW (about 15 minutes)

SECTION A: PICTURE CONVERSATION

You will be asked to talk about one of the photographs among the Interview Exercises at the back of this book. Your teacher will tell you which one of the photographs to look at.

SECTION B: READING PASSAGE

You will be asked to read aloud one of the reading passages among the Interview Exercises at the back of this book. Your teacher will tell you which one of the reading passages to look at.

SECTION C: STRUCTURED COMMUNICATION ACTIVITY

You will be asked to take part in a conversation with a group of other students or with your teacher. Your teacher will tell you which section among the Interview Exercises you should look at.

Interview Exercises

1

2

3

4

5

6

7

8

9

10

11 I'm not a reporter, but I am interested in talking to people when I'm visiting abroad and I'd like your views. You might call me an amateur politician, someone with an active concern over issues, especially health and safety issues. As it happens, we're a breed that my country produces in some quantity. But as you can guess, it makes life rather hectic when we start on each other.

12 I would attribute any success in my political career to the realisation that you learn more from your opponents than from your most fervent supporters. A politician's own associates will push him to disaster unless his enemies show him where the dangers are. If he is wise, he will often utter that old paradoxical prayer: God protect me from my friends.

[112]

13 The brain does so much at a subconscious level. For example, the eye changes its curvature to focus on distant objects or near ones, and it's not merely the lens but the pupil around that is self-adjusting. The miracle is that this delicate process goes on all the time and yet we are utterly unconscious of it. We in no way have to will it to happen.

14 I don't think you can blame the cat. All cats need exercise to sharpen their claws, and a cat kept in a city flat needs a special scratching post. Get one made, train your cat to use it (cats can be trained to understand commands), and it will expend its energies on the post and not on the furniture.

15 Within an hour of landing at the airport I was in a rickety old bus travelling across the delta. The journey took an hour and a half but the fare was the price of a sandwich and a cup of coffee back in New York. This trifling sum transported me, not just to another place but to another age; to a city that was old when our history was just beginning.

16 Do you think teachers and educational authorities have any real understanding of the sort of person the modern world needs? They could within two decades produce a generation that would transform the world. Their ideal of character is one that is completely anarchic. They admire most the sort of personality which would be most suitable for leading a gang of pirates.

17 Your Snack'n'Sandwich Toaster will quickly become an indispensable family asset, because its quality and sensible design features always result in a superb product. The toaster is designed to seal and cut your sandwiches in half automatically. You may care to notice the thermostat control, which not only saves you money but also gives golden brown sandwiches every time.

18   The sixties really were a phenomenal help to all of us, but they really followed, I think, the social revolution of the fifties when dramatists and other writers were actually changing the words that people were saying in the theatre and in the street. Then of course in the sixties youngsters for the first time had money. Physically things had changed.

19   In the wake of the civil disturbances in some of our inner city areas last year, attention has been given to the roles which national financial institutions and central and local government authorities might play in programmes designed to arrest the economic decay of such areas. We have taken an active role in a number of bodies which are working in areas of immediate concern.

20   He was a very nice man. I think the art is in total contradiction to the character of the man, because the art is really nasty. All those thorns and everything: it's all prickly, all persecuted, all conceived as disagreeable. . . I never thought the portraits very honest. I'm not at all sure that all those toads and beetles weren't the most natural expression of his interest in life. He didn't care for human beings at all.

21   This paragraph is from a newspaper article. Your partners have other paragraphs from the same article. Tell your partners about your part of the article in your own words and try to piece together the complete story.

> It has been rumoured in the City for some time that Arthur Hardwick's financial empire was on the verge of collapse and there have been allegations of an Income Tax Fraud.
> Mrs Hardwick, who separated from her husband six months ago, admitted that she had been worried for some time about her husband's mental state and feared he might take his own life. Mrs Hardwick is currently the constant companion of pop singer Johnnie Bull.

When you have found out about the other parts of the story, decide as a group how and why Mr Hardwick died.

22 Imagine that you and the other members of your group are members of a committee that is responsible for the planning of a party which your class is organising for 30 children aged between 7 and 9 from a local school. The agenda below shows the details that need to be decided on at this committee meeting.

CHILDREN'S PARTY COMMITTEE MEETING

Agenda

1 Food and drink (buffet-style): what needs to be bought and how is the food to be prepared and when is it to be served?
2 Entertainment: what sort of music, games and dancing would be suitable?
3 Supervision: how will the children be transported to and from the party and how will they be supervised during the time they are there?
4 Time and place: where and when should the party take place and how long should it last?

The examiner will tell you which items on the agenda you are responsible for. Be prepared to make a statement of your suggestions before you have a discussion with the other committee members.

23 'What could I have done?' Put yourself in the position of either King Claudius in *Hamlet* or Gabriel Oak in *Far From the Madding Crowd* and argue your case. Consider how a different course of action might have led to a happier outcome for you in the story.

24   Imagine that the examiner is thinking of
applying for a job in one of the
countries shown on the map.
What advice would you give, based on
the information shown below? What do
you think it would be like to live there?
Your partners have information about
the other countries on the map, so you
can ask them to tell you about the other
places.

THE
GAMBIA

GABON

SWAZILAND

THE GAMBIA
democratic republic,
  independent since 1965
Pop. 600,000
Capital: Banjul (40,000)
Life expectancy: M 39 F 43
  (UK: M 70 F 76)
Languages: English, Mandinka,
  Wolof
Per capita annual income: $250
  (UK: $7,920)
Economy: subsistence farming, peanuts for export, tourism (Northern
  Europeans)
Climate: warm dry winters, very hot and humid summers
Land: 11,000 sq km (half the size of Wales), in a narrow 300 km long
  strip on either side of the Gambia River

SENEGAL

Banjul

SENEGAL

25 Read this newspaper article and look at the instructions below.

TRAFFIC TROUBLES

The small market town of Mundham is buzzing with controversy this week after the announcement of government plans to build a bypass round the town. Most of the year traffic flows smoothly through the narrow streets of the town centre, but in July and August holiday traffic to the coast makes Mundham one of the country's worst bottlenecks. Last summer there were often 10km queues north and south of the town. A public meeting is to be held later this week, where local people will be able to give their views.

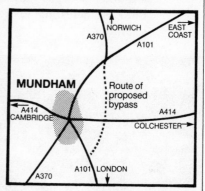

Imagine that you are a shopkeeper in Mundham. State your views on the proposal to bypass the town and give your reasons. Here are some ideas you may want to use:

Advantages of bypass: easier for local people to park and shop; easier for vans to deliver to shops; more pleasant for visitors to the town.

Disadvantages: less passing trade from motorists driving through; bypass only needed in summer; unnecessary cost.

Think of some ways in which the new road will favourably or adversely affect you *personally* as a shopkeeper and how it will affect your customers, family and fellow shopkeepers.

26 Look at the reproduction below of **'A Mother's Duties'**, painted by
Pieter de Hooch (1629–1682). You will have to describe it to your
partners in sufficient detail for them to build up a mental picture of it.
You must *not* show it to them, nor look at their pictures until the
examiner says you may. Later you will be expected to say what you
think is interesting, appealing or displeasing about each of the
paintings.

27   Read the news report below and then tell your partners about it in your own words. Tell them also what you think about the implications of the article and ask them for their comments.

Teacher stabbed

A TEACHER who caught an 18 year old pupil reading her neighbour's answer paper during an A-level exam had to be taken to hospital and given 24 stitches, Halesworth Crown Court was told yesterday.

Appearing as prosecution witness, Mr George Hall, 35, a mathematics teacher said that he tore up Mary Watson's answer paper and made her leave the examination room. As they reached the door, he said, she swore at him, drew a knife and stabbed him twice in the right arm.

Miss Watson, who denied the charges, told the court that she had lost her temper and shouted at Mr Hall but that she had used the knife to defend herself when Mr Hall tried to push her from the room. Miss Watson, who was forbidden to take any further examinations by the school's headmaster, said that her chances of being admitted to university were now slim.

The case was adjourned until Monday.

28   Look at these three opinions of politicians:
'Politicians are the same all over. They promise to build a bridge even where there's no river. '   (Nikita Khrushchev)
'I have come to the conclusion that politics are too serious a matter to be left to the politicians. '   (Charles de Gaulle)
'The more you read about politics, you've got to admit that each party is worse than the other. '   (Will Rogers)

Everybody seems to blame the politicians for what goes wrong in the world.
What do *you* think of them?
Would you like to be one? Give your reasons why or why not.
What are the qualities of a good politician?
Which politicians, past or present, do you admire most?

Prepare a short talk (no longer than a minute) to introduce your ideas. If you like, you can concentrate on just one of the questions asked above.

29   'Literature is more concerned with relationships between people than with stories or ideas.' To what extent do you agree with this view? How can it be applied to the text you have read? Give examples to support your views.

30 Imagine that you and your partners have decided to stay at one of the places described below. They are both in the same county and have been recommended by friends. Look at the information below, which you have noted down from an accommodation list. Your partners have information about the attractions of each hotel and about the area surrounding them. Tell your partners what you know about the hotels and find out what they know. Then discuss which hotel would suit you best for a week's stay in early summer.

EAST BAY HOTEL
14 twin-bedded rooms, 3 with bath, balcony and sea view.
£19 per person for bed, breakfast and evening meal.
(£3 extra per person for rooms with bath and balcony.)
In centre of East Bay village next to Fisherman's Arms Inn, short walk to sea.
Licensed restaurant but no bar in hotel.
Colour TV in lounge.

HINTON ARMS HOTEL
29 double, 3 single rooms, all with shower/toilet.
£24 per person (bed, breakfast and evening meal) or £19 (bed and breakfast).
2 km outside town on A30 trunk road.
3 restaurants, 2 bars, indoor pool, disco.

---

31   This paragraph is from a newspaper article. Your partners have other paragraphs from the same article. Tell your part of the story in your own words and decide together what the complete story is.

> Mystery still surrounds the death of Arthur Hardwick, the newspaper tycoon, who was found yesterday morning shot through the head in his London office at Green Park Towers.
>
> The body, which was discovered by a cleaner, was lying on the floor face down. A gun, recently fired and later identified as belonging to Mr Hardwick, was on his desk under a half-finished note to his estranged wife, Maureen.
>
> The note read: 'There is no point in our going on any longer. It is better to end it now . . .'

When you have found out about the other parts of the story, decide as a group how and why Mr Hardwick died.

32   Imagine that the examiner is thinking of applying for a job in one of the countries shown on the map.
What advice would you give, based on the information shown below? What do you think it would be like to live there? Your partners have information about the other countries on the map, so you can ask them to supply further advice.

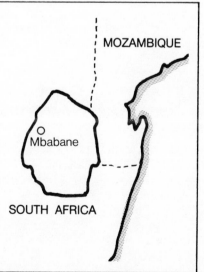

SWAZILAND
kingdom, independent since 1968
Pop. 580,000
Capital: Mbabane (22,000)
Life expectancy: M 44 F 48 (UK: M 70 F 76)
Languages: SiSwati, English
Per capita annual income: $680 (UK: $7,920)
Economy: mainly farming, exports of asbestos and iron ore, tourism (South Africans)
Climate: dry winters and wet summers; cool in the west and hot in the east
Land: 17,000 sq km (slightly smaller than Wales), mountains in the west and lowlands in the east

33 Read this newspaper article and look at the instructions below.

TRAFFIC TROUBLES

The small market town of Mundham is buzzing with controversy this week after the announcement of government plans to build a bypass round the town. Most of the year traffic flows smoothly through the narrow streets of the town centre, but in July and August holiday traffic to the coast makes Mundham one of the country's worst bottlenecks. Last summer there were often 10km queues north and south of the town. A public meeting is to be held later this week, where local people will be able to give their views.

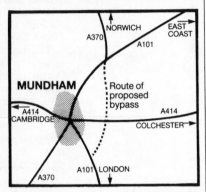

Imagine that you are a resident of the town living in the town centre. State your views on the ideas you may want to use:

Advantages of bypass: fewer accidents to pedestrians and children on cycles; less noise and pollution in the town.

Disadvantages: part of the cost will come from local taxes; the town may become a sleepy backwater.

Think of some ways in which the new road will affect you *personally* as a resident of the town and how it will affect your family and your neighbours.

34 Look at the reproduction below of **'The Last of England'**, painted by Ford Madox Brown (1821–93). You will have to describe it to your partners in sufficient detail for them to build up a mental picture of it. You must *not* show it to them, nor look at their pictures until the examiner says you may. Later you will have to discuss what you think is interesting, appealing or displeasing about each of the paintings.

35 Read the news report below and then tell your partners about it in your own words. Tell them also what you think about the implications of the article and ask them for their comments.

Hostess robbed

WINTON CROWN COURT was told yesterday about the theft of £5,000 in cash during a couple's weekend visit to a friend's house.

Mrs Gwen Poole told the court that she had invited Mr Edwin Williams and his wife Cheryl to spend the weekend at her home in Sussex after making friends with them during a summer holiday in Spain. "They seemed such a nice couple and we had a really wonderful time together in Benidorm. It was only after they had left my home that I found all my money was missing. It was my life's savings and now I have nothing.

By the time the police caught up with them, they had spent nearly all the money and only about £200 was left."

Mr and Mrs Williams both pleaded guilty to the offence of theft. Mr Williams received a six month sentence, suspended for two years, and his wife received a three month sentence, suspended for one year.

36

The price was £12,000

Imagine that the above sentence is the headline of a news report *or* the last line of a short story. You have a few moments to think of *your* version of the story before you tell it to your group (or to the examiner). You may make some brief notes if you wish to help you remember the story you are going to tell.

Listen to and comment on the other candidates' versions of the story and ask them questions too, if you wish.

37 What insights does the text you have read give you into the life and character of the writer's country and into the period he or she is writing about?

What relevance does the text have to present-day concerns and interests?

38 Imagine that you and your partners have decided to stay at one of the hotels described below. They are both in the same county and have been recommended by friends. Look at the information below, which you have been given by friends who have stayed there. Your partners have information about the prices and facilities and about the area surrounding each hotel. Tell your partners what you know and find out what they know. Then discuss which hotel would suit you best for a week's stay in early summer.

EAST BAY HOTEL

Rooms simply furnished. Some with sea view but most look out over village. No TV in rooms.
Family-run hotel (Mr and Mrs Hancock and three daughters). They do all the cooking, serving etc. (seem unfriendly, but very helpful and kind once you get to know them). Food plain but plentiful. Fresh vegetables, emphasis on traditional English fare.

HINTON ARMS HOTEL

Rooms small but comfortable. Rooms at front of hotel noisy (traffic). All have b/w TV.
Part of Windward chain of 50 hotels. Service sometimes poor at busy times (summer weekends attract passing motorists).
Half-board rate includes simple set meal in the Buttery Restaurant, but not in French Bistro (expensive), or Steak Bar. Food not wonderful but reasonably good.

---

39 This paragraph is from a newspaper article. Your partners have other paragraphs from the same article. Tell your part of the story in your own words and decide together what the complete story is.

> Arthur Hardwick began his career as a street trader when he left school at 15. Within 10 years he was the owner of a chain of South London supermarkets with a turnover of £5 million.
>
> After selling his stores to Tesco he invested in the newspaper business and became the chairman of Fleetwood Press where he was largely responsible for the launching of the highly successful 'Daily Globe'.
>
> Shortly before this he had succeeded in having all members of the Fleetwood family removed from the board of directors. Fleetwood Press was renamed the Hardwick Organisation after Eric Fleetwood's unsuccessful attempt to regain control of the company in 1979. Eric Fleetwood's recent critical biography of Mr Hardwick brought their rivalry back into the public eye last year.

When you have found out about the other parts of the story, decide as a group how and why Mr Hardwick died.

40 Imagine that the examiner is thinking of applying for a job in one of the countries shown on the map. What advice would you give, based on the information shown below? What do you think it would be like to live there? Your partners have information about the other countries on the map, so you can ask them to supply further advice.

GABON
democratic republic, independent since 1960
Pop: 1.23 million
Capital: Libreville (250,000)
Life expectancy: M 42 F 45 (UK: M 70 F 76)
Languages: French, Fang
Per capita annual income: $3,680 (UK: $7,920)
Economy: oil, manganese, uranium, iron ore exported but 85% of people work in agriculture, fishing and forestry
Climate: very hot and humid all year
Land: 270,000 sq km (about the size of the UK), mainly tropical rain forest and mountains

41 Read this newspaper article and look at the instructions below.

TRAFFIC TROUBLES

The small market town of Mundham is buzzing with controversy this week after the announcement of government plans to build a bypass round the town. Most of the year traffic flows smoothly through the narrow streets of the town centre, but in July and August holiday traffic to the coast makes Mundham one of the country's worst bottlenecks. Last summer there were often 10km queues north and south of the town. A public meeting is to be held later this week, where local people will be able to give their views.

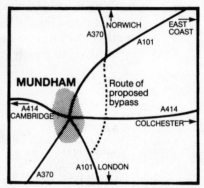

Imagine that you live in the countryside just outside Mundham. State your views on the proposal to bypass the town and give your reasons. Here are some ideas you may want to use:

Advantages of bypass: it will be easier to get into the town to shop; the town will be more pleasant and quiet.

Disadvantages: the proposed route crosses fertile agricultural land; some beautiful scenery will be ruined by the new road.

Think of some ways in which the new road will affect you *personally* as a local countryman or woman and how it will affect your neighbours and your family.

42 Look at the reproduction below of **'The Menaced Assassin'**, painted
by René Magritte (1898–1967). You will have to describe it to your
partners in sufficient detail for them to build up a mental picture of it.
You must *not* show it to them, nor must you look at their pictures
until the examiner says you may. Later you will have to discuss what
you find interesting, appealing or displeasing about the three
paintings.

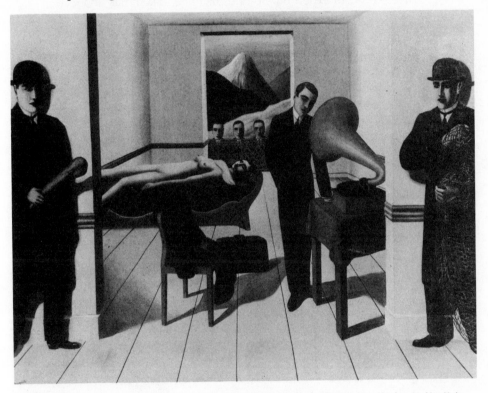

MAGRITTE, René *The Menaced Assassin* (1926). Oil on canvas, 150.4 × 195.2 cm. Collection, The Museum of Modern Art, New York.
Kay Sage Tanguy Fund.

43 Read the news report below and then tell your partners about it in
your own words. Tell them also what you think about the
implications of the article and ask them for their comments.

Finding and keeping

AFTER FINDING a handbag containing
£25, credit cards and personal effects on
his bus, Doncaster Transport conductor
Donald Taylor helped himself to £20 and
handed the bag and its contents in to the
lost property office, South Yorkshire magistrates were told.

Accused of stealing the money, Mr
Taylor, 41, denied the charge and told
magistrates that the owner of the bag, Mrs
J. Forbes, must have made a mistake about
the sum of money she had left in her bag.

Mr Taylor, who has lost his job as bus
conductor and is now unemployed, was
found guilty and fined £120.

44 Imagine that you have to describe the modern world to someone who has just been rescued after being alone on a desert island for the last fifty years. Decide with your partners how you would describe *either* TV and video *or* modern aircraft and airports.

Imagine that the person you will be talking to is going to use video equipment (or travel by plane and use airport facilities). You do not need to be an expert on either topic to be able to talk about it.

45 How is the text you have read typical of its *genre* (tragedy, historical novel, short story collection, etc.)?
How does it stand out as an exceptional example of the *genre* and what makes it particularly 'special' or 'great'?
What ideas do you think the writer is trying to get across in this particular story (or collection)?

46 Imagine that you and your partners have decided to stay at one of the places described below. They are both in the same county and have been recommended by friends. Look at the information below, which you have noted down from a guide book. Your partners have information about the prices, facilities and attractions of a hotel in each place. Tell your partners what you know about the places and find out what they know. Then discuss which hotel would suit you best for a week's stay in early summer.

> EAST BAY
> Isolated fishing village, popular with summer visitors.
> 20 km from nearest town.
> Shingle beach (pebbles) with high cliffs. Safe bathing at low tide.
> Inland: rather flat countryside with some good walks.
> Nearby: Sutton Heath Nature Reserve (rare ducks and other water birds), Glenville Hall (stately home of Lord Glenville, open August only).
>
> HINTON
> Small market town in dairy farming area. 10 km from historic city of Southchester, 35 km from nearest beaches (sandy).
> Undulating countryside with lovely walks beside nearby River Trent (fishing).
> Nearby: Woodlands Country Park, Hindley Manor Safari Park (lions and giraffes), Hinton House and gardens (open all year).

47 Have you seen a film or TV version of the text you have read? If so, how did it do justice to the text? What was left out and what needed to be added to make the text into a film? How did the film handle the story and its setting, characters and dialogue?

If you have not seen a film version of the text you have read, what do you think such a film would be like? What would have to be left out or added to make it into a film? Could such a film do justice to the story and its setting, characters and dialogue?

Acknowledgements

The University of Cambridge Local Examinations Syndicate and the publishers are grateful to the following for permission to reproduce texts and illustrations. It has not been possible to identify sources of all the material used and in such cases the publishers would welcome information from copyright owners.

Pergamon Press Ltd for the extract on pp. 23–24 from 'Wings over Everest' by D. F. McIntyre in *Open the Sky* by E. M. Quittendin; The Bodley Head Ltd for the extract on p. 25 from 'The Mark-2 Wife' in *The Ballroom of Romance and other stories* by William Trevor; Five Arches Press for the extract from *Walking the Pembrokeshire Coast Path* by Patrick Stark on p. 26; Collins Publishers for the extract from *Leakey's Luck* by Sonia Cole on p. 67; John Carter and *Good Housekeeping* for the extract on pp. 87–88; Sally and Richard Greenhill for photographs on pp. 107, 108 and 109; Jeremy Pembrey for photographs on pp. 108–112; Rijksmuseum – Stichting for Pieter de Hooch's 'A Mother's Duties' on p. 118; Birmingham Museums and Art Gallery for Ford Madox Brown's 'The Last of England' on p. 123; The Museum of Modern Art, New York for René Magritte's 'The Menaced Assassin' on p. 129.

Drawings by Chris Evans. Artwork by Grafton Graphics.

UNIVERSITY OF CAMBRIDGE
LOCAL EXAMINATIONS SYNDICATE

Answer Sheet

PAPER 1   READING COMPREHENSION

NAME ....

PLEASE READ THESE NOTES CAREFULLY
1. Check that this answer sheet has your correct name and index number printed on it.

2. For each question, suggested answers are given on your question paper. CHOOSE ONE LETTER ONLY for each question, and show your choice clearly ON THIS SHEET.

MARK HEAVILY

EXAMPLE: If you think B is the right letter for Question 1, fill in the answer sheet like this

A ○   B ●   C ○   D ○

FILL IN THE LOZENGES

3. **USE ORDINARY PENCIL ONLY** (SOFT-2B or GRADE 1 PREFERRED)
    Any errors must be thoroughly rubbed out using a clean eraser.

	A	B	C	D			A	B	C	D			A	B	C	D
1	○	○	○	○		16	○	○	○	○		31	○	○	○	○
2	○	○	○	○		17	○	○	○	○		32	○	○	○	○
3	○	○	○	○		18	○	○	○	○		33	○	○	○	○
4	○	○	○	○		19	○	○	○	○		34	○	○	○	○
5	○	○	○	○		20	○	○	○	○		35	○	○	○	○
6	○	○	○	○		21	○	○	○	○		36	○	○	○	○
7	○	○	○	○		22	○	○	○	○		37	○	○	○	○
8	○	○	○	○		23	○	○	○	○		38	○	○	○	○
9	○	○	○	○		24	○	○	○	○		39	○	○	○	○
10	○	○	○	○		25	○	○	○	○		40	○	○	○	○
11	○	○	○	○		26	○	○	○	○						
12	○	○	○	○		27	○	○	○	○						
13	○	○	○	○		28	○	○	○	○						
14	○	○	○	○		29	○	○	○	○						
15	○	○	○	○		30	○	○	○	○						

SHOW YOUR ANSWERS ON THIS SHEET   **USE PENCIL ONLY**

UNIVERSITY OF CAMBRIDGE
LOCAL EXAMINATIONS SYNDICATE

Answer Sheet

PAPER 1   READING COMPREHENSION

NAME ....

PLEASE READ THESE NOTES CAREFULLY

1. Check that this answer sheet has your correct name and index number printed on it.

2. For each question, suggested answers are given on your question paper. CHOOSE ONE LETTER ONLY for each question, and show your choice clearly ON THIS SHEET.

MARK HEAVILY

EXAMPLE: If you think B is the right letter for Question 1, fill in the answer sheet like this

A ⏚   B ⬤   C ⏚   D ⏚

FILL IN THE LOZENGES

3. **USE ORDINARY PENCIL ONLY** (SOFT-2B or GRADE 1 PREFERRED)
   Any errors must be thoroughly rubbed out using a clean eraser.

	A B C D		A B C D		A B C D
1	⏚ ⏚ ⏚ ⏚	16	⏚ ⏚ ⏚ ⏚	31	⏚ ⏚ ⏚ ⏚
2	⏚ ⏚ ⏚ ⏚	17	⏚ ⏚ ⏚ ⏚	32	⏚ ⏚ ⏚ ⏚
3	⏚ ⏚ ⏚ ⏚	18	⏚ ⏚ ⏚ ⏚	33	⏚ ⏚ ⏚ ⏚
4	⏚ ⏚ ⏚ ⏚	19	⏚ ⏚ ⏚ ⏚	34	⏚ ⏚ ⏚ ⏚
5	⏚ ⏚ ⏚ ⏚	20	⏚ ⏚ ⏚ ⏚	35	⏚ ⏚ ⏚ ⏚
6	⏚ ⏚ ⏚ ⏚	21	⏚ ⏚ ⏚ ⏚	36	⏚ ⏚ ⏚ ⏚
7	⏚ ⏚ ⏚ ⏚	22	⏚ ⏚ ⏚ ⏚	37	⏚ ⏚ ⏚ ⏚
8	⏚ ⏚ ⏚ ⏚	23	⏚ ⏚ ⏚ ⏚	38	⏚ ⏚ ⏚ ⏚
9	⏚ ⏚ ⏚ ⏚	24	⏚ ⏚ ⏚ ⏚	39	⏚ ⏚ ⏚ ⏚
10	⏚ ⏚ ⏚ ⏚	25	⏚ ⏚ ⏚ ⏚	40	⏚ ⏚ ⏚ ⏚
11	⏚ ⏚ ⏚ ⏚	26	⏚ ⏚ ⏚ ⏚		
12	⏚ ⏚ ⏚ ⏚	27	⏚ ⏚ ⏚ ⏚		
13	⏚ ⏚ ⏚ ⏚	28	⏚ ⏚ ⏚ ⏚		
14	⏚ ⏚ ⏚ ⏚	29	⏚ ⏚ ⏚ ⏚		
15	⏚ ⏚ ⏚ ⏚	30	⏚ ⏚ ⏚ ⏚		

SHOW YOUR ANSWERS ON THIS SHEET   **USE PENCIL ONLY**

UNIVERSITY OF CAMBRIDGE
LOCAL EXAMINATIONS SYNDICATE

Answer Sheet

PAPER 1   READING COMPREHENSION

NAME ....

PLEASE READ THESE NOTES CAREFULLY

1.   Check that this answer sheet has your correct name and index number printed on it.

2.   For each question, suggested answers are given on your question paper. CHOOSE ONE LETTER ONLY for each question, and show your choice clearly ON THIS SHEET.

MARK HEAVILY

EXAMPLE: If you think B is the right letter for Question 1, fill in the answer sheet like this

A ⊖   B ⬤   C ⊖   D ⊖

FILL IN THE LOZENGES

---

3.   **USE ORDINARY PENCIL ONLY** (SOFT - 2B or GRADE 1 PREFERRED)
Any errors must be thoroughly rubbed out using a clean eraser.

	A	B	C	D		A	B	C	D		A	B	C	D
1	⊖	⊖	⊖	⊖	16	⊖	⊖	⊖	⊖	31	⊖	⊖	⊖	⊖
2	⊖	⊖	⊖	⊖	17	⊖	⊖	⊖	⊖	32	⊖	⊖	⊖	⊖
3	⊖	⊖	⊖	⊖	18	⊖	⊖	⊖	⊖	33	⊖	⊖	⊖	⊖
4	⊖	⊖	⊖	⊖	19	⊖	⊖	⊖	⊖	34	⊖	⊖	⊖	⊖
5	⊖	⊖	⊖	⊖	20	⊖	⊖	⊖	⊖	35	⊖	⊖	⊖	⊖
6	⊖	⊖	⊖	⊖	21	⊖	⊖	⊖	⊖	36	⊖	⊖	⊖	⊖
7	⊖	⊖	⊖	⊖	22	⊖	⊖	⊖	⊖	37	⊖	⊖	⊖	⊖
8	⊖	⊖	⊖	⊖	23	⊖	⊖	⊖	⊖	38	⊖	⊖	⊖	⊖
9	⊖	⊖	⊖	⊖	24	⊖	⊖	⊖	⊖	39	⊖	⊖	⊖	⊖
10	⊖	⊖	⊖	⊖	25	⊖	⊖	⊖	⊖	40	⊖	⊖	⊖	⊖
11	⊖	⊖	⊖	⊖	26	⊖	⊖	⊖	⊖					
12	⊖	⊖	⊖	⊖	27	⊖	⊖	⊖	⊖					
13	⊖	⊖	⊖	⊖	28	⊖	⊖	⊖	⊖					
14	⊖	⊖	⊖	⊖	29	⊖	⊖	⊖	⊖					
15	⊖	⊖	⊖	⊖	30	⊖	⊖	⊖	⊖					

SHOW YOUR ANSWERS ON THIS SHEET   USE PENCIL ONLY

UNIVERSITY OF CAMBRIDGE
LOCAL EXAMINATIONS SYNDICATE

Answer Sheet

PAPER 1   READING COMPREHENSION

NAME ....

PLEASE READ THESE NOTES CAREFULLY

1. Check that this answer sheet has your correct name and index number printed on it.

2. For each question, suggested answers are given on your question paper. CHOOSE ONE LETTER ONLY for each question, and show your choice clearly ON THIS SHEET.

MARK HEAVILY

EXAMPLE: If you think B is the right letter for Question 1, fill in the answer sheet like this

A ◯   B ●   C ◯   D ◯

FILL IN THE LOZENGES

---

3. **USE ORDINARY PENCIL ONLY** (SOFT-2B or GRADE 1 PREFERRED)
    Any errors must be thoroughly rubbed out using a clean eraser.

	A	B	C	D			A	B	C	D			A	B	C	D
1	◯	◯	◯	◯		16	◯	◯	◯	◯		31	◯	◯	◯	◯
2	◯	◯	◯	◯		17	◯	◯	◯	◯		32	◯	◯	◯	◯
3	◯	◯	◯	◯		18	◯	◯	◯	◯		33	◯	◯	◯	◯
4	◯	◯	◯	◯		19	◯	◯	◯	◯		34	◯	◯	◯	◯
5	◯	◯	◯	◯		20	◯	◯	◯	◯		35	◯	◯	◯	◯
6	◯	◯	◯	◯		21	◯	◯	◯	◯		36	◯	◯	◯	◯
7	◯	◯	◯	◯		22	◯	◯	◯	◯		37	◯	◯	◯	◯
8	◯	◯	◯	◯		23	◯	◯	◯	◯		38	◯	◯	◯	◯
9	◯	◯	◯	◯		24	◯	◯	◯	◯		39	◯	◯	◯	◯
10	◯	◯	◯	◯		25	◯	◯	◯	◯		40	◯	◯	◯	◯
11	◯	◯	◯	◯		26	◯	◯	◯	◯						
12	◯	◯	◯	◯		27	◯	◯	◯	◯						
13	◯	◯	◯	◯		28	◯	◯	◯	◯						
14	◯	◯	◯	◯		29	◯	◯	◯	◯						
15	◯	◯	◯	◯		30	◯	◯	◯	◯						

SHOW YOUR ANSWERS ON THIS SHEET   **USE PENCIL ONLY**

UNIVERSITY OF CAMBRIDGE
LOCAL EXAMINATIONS SYNDICATE

Answer Sheet

PAPER 1   READING COMPREHENSION

NAME ....

PLEASE READ THESE NOTES CAREFULLY

1.   Check that this answer sheet has your correct name and index number printed on it.

2.   For each question, suggested answers are given on your question paper. CHOOSE ONE LETTER ONLY
     for each question, and show your choice clearly ON THIS SHEET.

**MARK
HEAVILY**

EXAMPLE: If you think B is the right letter for Question 1,
fill in the answer sheet like this

    A   B   C   D

**FILL IN
THE
LOZENGES**

3.   **USE ORDINARY PENCIL ONLY** (SOFT-2B or GRADE 1 PREFERRED)
     Any errors must be thoroughly rubbed out using a clean eraser.

	A	B	C	D			A	B	C	D			A	B	C	D
1	◯	◯	◯	◯		16	◯	◯	◯	◯		31	◯	◯	◯	◯
2	◯	◯	◯	◯		17	◯	◯	◯	◯		32	◯	◯	◯	◯
3	◯	◯	◯	◯		18	◯	◯	◯	◯		33	◯	◯	◯	◯
4	◯	◯	◯	◯		19	◯	◯	◯	◯		34	◯	◯	◯	◯
5	◯	◯	◯	◯		20	◯	◯	◯	◯		35	◯	◯	◯	◯
6	◯	◯	◯	◯		21	◯	◯	◯	◯		36	◯	◯	◯	◯
7	◯	◯	◯	◯		22	◯	◯	◯	◯		37	◯	◯	◯	◯
8	◯	◯	◯	◯		23	◯	◯	◯	◯		38	◯	◯	◯	◯
9	◯	◯	◯	◯		24	◯	◯	◯	◯		39	◯	◯	◯	◯
10	◯	◯	◯	◯		25	◯	◯	◯	◯		40	◯	◯	◯	◯
11	◯	◯	◯	◯		26	◯	◯	◯	◯						
12	◯	◯	◯	◯		27	◯	◯	◯	◯						
13	◯	◯	◯	◯		28	◯	◯	◯	◯						
14	◯	◯	◯	◯		29	◯	◯	◯	◯						
15	◯	◯	◯	◯		30	◯	◯	◯	◯						

SHOW YOUR ANSWERS ON THIS SHEET   **USE PENCIL ONLY**

UNIVERSITY OF CAMBRIDGE
LOCAL EXAMINATIONS SYNDICATE

Answer Sheet

PAPER 1   READING COMPREHENSION

NAME ....

PLEASE READ THESE NOTES CAREFULLY

1. Check that this answer sheet has your correct name and index number printed on it.

2. For each question, suggested answers are given on your question paper. CHOOSE ONE LETTER ONLY for each question, and show your choice clearly ON THIS SHEET.

MARK HEAVILY

EXAMPLE: If you think B is the right letter for Question 1, fill in the answer sheet like this

A ◯   B ●   C ◯   D ◯

FILL IN THE LOZENGES

---

3. **USE ORDINARY PENCIL ONLY** (SOFT - 2B or GRADE 1 PREFERRED)
    Any errors must be thoroughly rubbed out using a clean eraser.

1	A ◯ B ◯ C ◯ D ◯	16	A ◯ B ◯ C ◯ D ◯	31	A ◯ B ◯ C ◯ D ◯
2	A ◯ B ◯ C ◯ D ◯	17	A ◯ B ◯ C ◯ D ◯	32	A ◯ B ◯ C ◯ D ◯
3	A ◯ B ◯ C ◯ D ◯	18	A ◯ B ◯ C ◯ D ◯	33	A ◯ B ◯ C ◯ D ◯
4	A ◯ B ◯ C ◯ D ◯	19	A ◯ B ◯ C ◯ D ◯	34	A ◯ B ◯ C ◯ D ◯
5	A ◯ B ◯ C ◯ D ◯	20	A ◯ B ◯ C ◯ D ◯	35	A ◯ B ◯ C ◯ D ◯
6	A ◯ B ◯ C ◯ D ◯	21	A ◯ B ◯ C ◯ D ◯	36	A ◯ B ◯ C ◯ D ◯
7	A ◯ B ◯ C ◯ D ◯	22	A ◯ B ◯ C ◯ D ◯	37	A ◯ B ◯ C ◯ D ◯
8	A ◯ B ◯ C ◯ D ◯	23	A ◯ B ◯ C ◯ D ◯	38	A ◯ B ◯ C ◯ D ◯
9	A ◯ B ◯ C ◯ D ◯	24	A ◯ B ◯ C ◯ D ◯	39	A ◯ B ◯ C ◯ D ◯
10	A ◯ B ◯ C ◯ D ◯	25	A ◯ B ◯ C ◯ D ◯	40	A ◯ B ◯ C ◯ D ◯
11	A ◯ B ◯ C ◯ D ◯	26	A ◯ B ◯ C ◯ D ◯		
12	A ◯ B ◯ C ◯ D ◯	27	A ◯ B ◯ C ◯ D ◯		
13	A ◯ B ◯ C ◯ D ◯	28	A ◯ B ◯ C ◯ D ◯		
14	A ◯ B ◯ C ◯ D ◯	29	A ◯ B ◯ C ◯ D ◯		
15	A ◯ B ◯ C ◯ D ◯	30	A ◯ B ◯ C ◯ D ◯		

SHOW YOUR ANSWERS ON THIS SHEET   **USE PENCIL ONLY**